Lady for the Defense

LADY
FOR THE
DEFENSE

A Biography of Belva Lockwood

MARY VIRGINIA FOX

Harcourt Brace Jovanovich

New York and London

Frontispiece portrait of Belva Lockwood by
Nellie Mathes Horne, courtesy of the National Portrait
Gallery, Smithsonian Institution, Washington, D.C.

Library of Congress Cataloging in Publication Data

Fox, Mary Virginia.
Lady for the defense.

Bibliography: p.
SUMMARY: A biography of the first woman lawyer to
practice before the United States Supreme Court who also
was the first woman candidate for President.
1. Lockwood, Belva Ann Bennett, 1830–1917—Juvenile
literature.   [1. Lockwood, Belva Ann Bennett, 1830–1917.
2. Lawyers]   I. Title.
KF368.L58F69   340'.092'4 [B] [92]   74-27460
ISBN 0-15-243400-3

To my sister

Leila Merrell Foster,

M. Div., J.D., Ph.D.,

of whom

Belva would have been very proud

Contents

PART I

"If One Dreams Sensibly—"

One

The rain had turned to sleet, which sheathed the branches of the sugar maple with icy fingers. Belva turned and twisted in her little bed tucked under the slant of the cabin's roof. Only inches above her head the tree branches scratched and clawed at the cedar shingles. She burrowed a little deeper in her quilt cocoon and hugged the covers close to her ears to shut out the noise of the storm.

Down below, the cooking fire gave off a smoky warmth that seeped through the cracks in the loft floor. Mama and Papa and four-year-old Cyrene slept in the family room. The house was built of timbers, hand hewn from virgin stands of oak found in abundance in these hills of western New York State in 1838. The squared logs had been carefully planed to fit a neat pattern, and the seams had been caulked with mud plaster, but until spring split the creek open and feathered the leaves a pale green, the house would never be warm enough for real comfort. Belva usually didn't mind. There were always bundling clothes to cheat the cold, but she hated the wind that thrashed the trees about and piled the snow in freakish peaks and swirls.

Belva looked across the "up-the-ladder room" toward Rachel's bed. It was too dark to see her older sister's face, but she could hear Rachel's steady breathing. The storm hadn't bothered her a bit. Papa often teased, "Rachel will sleep through her wedding day if we don't wake her."

Six-year-old Warren's cot was in the far corner. He had hunched so far under the covers that only a mound of comforters showed where he was sleeping.

Suddenly an overloaded branch snapped like a gun shot and shattered its glassy coat in a splintering crash against the roof and onto the ground. Warren's heap of covers heaved up, and a tousled head of hair appeared. "Mama, Mama," he cried.

"Don't cry, Warrie," Belva whispered. "It's just a dead branch that fell. Think how much fun it will be in the morning to pick up the icicles and dip them in the sugar pots."

Belva was only two years older than Warren, but she watched after him and mothered him more than Rachel, who had no patience with baby brothers.

"But it's Sammy. I hear her on the roof."

Samantha, called Sammy by all the Bennetts, was a big calico cat with slanting amber eyes.

"It's just the icy branches hitting the roof, Warrie. Listen."

Just then Belva heard a different noise. She sat up in bed, straining to hear it again. Yes, it was a cat meowing.

"You hear, you hear?" wailed Warren. "I couldn't find her after supper last night. Then I forgot about her when I went to bed."

Again there was a mewing. "Belva we've gotta get her. She may be having her kittens right now."

Belva nodded. "She must be on the roof by the dormer."

Quickly she slipped out of bed. The floor was cold against her bare feet, but she didn't bother to slip on her winter "leathers." The four tiny panes of the attic dormer were frosted over, so she could see nothing outside. She strained to open the window a crack. She hoped Sammy had found protection on the ledge just below the windowsill, but all she could see was a sheet of ice and part of the maple branch that had caught on the overhang.

She opened the sash further. The wind whipped a spray of rain and sleet against her face. She pulled back and shut the window quickly to keep out the storm.

"Belva, we've gotta do something." Warren was out of his bed. Tears filled his eyes. "It's my fault. I should've brought her in."

"Sh, be quiet. I'm going to put on my clothes and climb out. You can shut the window behind me."

"Belva, you can't. Papa wouldn't let you."

"Just you stay by the window and don't bother Papa or Mama about anything. I've climbed the roof before. You know it. Who gets to the top of the apple tree in the summer, remember?"

"But it's dark out there."

Belva put on her woolen petticoat over her nightdress and her heavy homespun coat over that. Should she wear her shoes? They'd slip, and she'd have to feel for every edge of support if she had to crawl far from the window ledge.

Warren was too frightened to say anything more. He obediently stood guard by the window. Once again they heard the faint meow of the cat. Belva pulled up the sash as far as it would go and edged her way out to the sill that cut a flat plane into the sloping roof. Warren closed the window behind her.

Belva was alone. The noise of the storm thundered around her. The big maple slashed its branches against each other, breaking off hunks of ice that fell to the ground like broken glass. The sleet stung her eyes. She squinted against the black sky but could see no trace of Sammy's brown and black and white coat.

"Sammy, Sammy, where are you?" Belva called again and again. She was angry now. "This is no time to be playing games. You know you shouldn't be on the roof."

Almost immediately she was answered by a wailing meow.

"You come down here this minute," called Belva.

Now she could dimly make out the spotted form of Sammy as she straddled the ridge pole close to the stone chimney. In her mouth she carried a fuzzy form.

"Oh, Sammy, is that your kitten? Wait right there. I'll come get you."

Belva talked to the cat as if Sammy could understand every word of her instructions, and maybe Sammy did understand, Belva thought. The cat sat down by her chimney perch and waited.

Carefully Belva reached out and groped for a handhold, a warped shingle, an extra heavy one that would give her some support, but the roof was glazed with an inch coating of smooth ice. It was no use. No one could climb that unbroken surface.

"Oh, Sammy, Sammy," she cried.

She was about to turn back when suddenly her fingers felt a wet piece of wood that jutted free from the ice. And here was another and another. The big branch of the maple had plowed a path clear of ice as it had slammed against the house and to the ground.

Carefully, slowly, Belva reached out her right foot to gain a toehold. She put her weight against a rough shingle. Leaning against the slanting roof, she pushed herself up a few inches. Reaching up again her hand caught something rough, solid. She held on as her left foot found another support to push against. Her hands and feet were numb, her body soaked to the skin, but she kept talking to the cat.

"I'm coming, Sammy. Don't worry. Just a minute more. Just a few feet more."

She spoke the words to keep up her own courage. She had never realized the roof was so high, so steep, but just above her head was the chimney. Her hand touched the rough stone. It was warm from the hearth fire below. Sammy had found a good place to hide from the storm.

The cat stretched herself out of the wedge of protection. She held her kitten gently in her mouth by the nap of its neck. Belva placed her hand at the back of Sammy's neck. Grabbing a handful of wet fur, she tried to lift the cat toward her. As Sammy's claws pulled loose from the cedar shingles, she slipped into Belva's arms and clutched at her sleeve. The frightened kitten mewed.

"There now, you'll be warm and dry soon," Belva said soothingly.

She placed Sammy inside her coat and gently took the tiny kitten. "Don't worry, Sammy. I'll put your kitten in my pocket so we won't drop her on the way down. We'll be out of the weather in a minute."

But it was longer than that before she could inch her way back to the safety of the window ledge. Warren was peering with frightened eyes out of a circle of glass he had cleared of frost. Quickly he opened the window wide, and Belva stumbled into the room. Her frozen hands were shaking, so that it was hard for her to unbutton her coat, but Sammy leaped from her side and meowed loudly for the return of her kitten. Belva reached into her pocket and pulled out the soft curl of sleek wet fur that was just now beginning to fluff into a gray kitten shape.

"Th-thank you, Belva," Warren stammered. "You were brave to climb out there."

"Somebody had to," said Belva.

"I should have. Boys are supposed to be braver, but I was scared."

"Nonsense, Warrie. You take Sammy and her kitten downstairs to her box, but be quiet about it and don't wake up the family."

Belva took off her wet clothes and climbed into her bed of quilts. Her feet felt like two blocks of ice, and she could barely move her fingers. Here and there the ice had cut into them, but she could feel nothing. She hugged her knees to her chest and buried her head under the covers to breathe some warmth into her body. Just as the night sky lightened to show strips of ragged clouds, Belva fell asleep.

It seemed only minutes later when she was awakened by the thud of a chunk of wood as Mama stoked the kitchen fire below. Usually the family had half an hour more of squinting, stretching sleep before being called for Saturday breakfast, but Belva slipped out of bed as soon as she opened her eyes. She must see how Sammy and the kitten were.

Hurriedly she put on her chore clothes. She had to fold up the waistband of her skirt and roll a cuff in her sweater. They were Rachel's hand-me-downs, but Belva was so much smaller than her ten-year-old sister that she usually wore out her clothes before they really fit. Rachel, even now, could look like a young lady, especially when she coiled her thick black hair queenlike on top of her head. Belva knew her own pale braids could never frame the face of a princess. Her nose was a bit too sharp, and the skin of her face stretched taut over her cheekbones, "pinched," some had said, but Belva kept telling herself it didn't matter much. She could do a lot more things than Rachel could, like riding horses and climbing trees.

The only trouble with Rachel was that she had the airs of the oldest of the family, who deemed it right and proper to give advice on almost any subject when parents weren't around.

"Mind your manners, Belva."

"Warrie, slick down your hair."

Rachel was still sleeping soundly, so Belva didn't worry that she had put on a good sweater with her patched skirt. She scurried down the ladder-stairs. There in the box with Sammy was not just one gray ball of fur, but four kittens of assorted colors.

"Oh, Mama, look. Aren't they adorable?"

Mrs. Bennett put down the wooden spoon with which she was stirring the porridge. She had the sharp features, pale hair, and the reed-thin body of her younger daughter. She smiled as she looked at the peaceful family.

"There she is taking care of her kittens all by herself. She's one cat who surely doesn't cause trouble."

Belva said nothing. If the truth were known, Belva knew Sammy could cause plenty of trouble for her.

"Can she have some milk, Mama?"

"I've already poured some by the sink pump."

Warren had heard voices. Now he joined them in the kitchen by the kitten box.

"It's strange to have you both up so early on a Saturday," said Mama. "You must have known Sammy had a surprise for you."

Warren looked at her sister, but Belva put her finger to her mouth to warn for silence. It wasn't until everyone was seated before the trestle table with its porridge bowls and muffin basket that questions were asked. Belva was reaching for the syrup pitcher when her mother saw the cuts on her hand.

"Why, Belva, whatever happened to you?"

Belva drew back her hand hurriedly and hid it in her lap. "Just a scratch, Mama."

"It's more than that. Let me see."

Belva timidly held up her hand again. A red line circled her thumb and another etched her wrist.

"Those are bad cuts. Let me bandage that for you. But Belva, how did it happen?" Mama asked anxiously.

"I was getting the cat," Belva answered, keeping her eyes on the table.

"Better stay away from Sammy while she's protecting her family," Papa added.

"It wasn't Sammy's fault at all. It was my fault," Warrie shouted nervously. He was almost in tears again. Belva frowned and looked at him hard.

"Now what did happen?" Mr. Bennett put down his spoon and looked gravely from Warren to Belva.

Warren's words tumbled out. "I forgot to bring her in last night and she climbed up by the chimney and she was having her kittens and Belva had to climb on the roof to get her."

"Last night in the storm?" Mama asked in alarm.

Belva nodded silently.

"Why, Belva, how terrible. You should never have done such a thing. You might have caught your death of cold." Mama rose and put her hand on her daughter's head. "Feverish, I'm sure of it. You'll stay in bed today and dose with camphor."

"But, Mama, I am all right, really."

"You'll do as your mother says, Belva," Papa ordered. "You could have had a serious fall, something that even your mother's camphorated oil could never have cured."

"I told you it was my fault," Warren interrupted. "I should have been the one to get Sammy, but I was scared."

Belva was angry. She didn't know exactly why, but she wished everyone would stop making such a fuss about nothing. She turned to Warren with a frown. "I don't know why boys are supposed to be any braver than girls. There's almost nothing a girl can't do as well as a boy when she's given a chance."

"I'll not start on that argument again now," said Papa, "but one thing for certain, you will not try to prove it by climbing any more roofs."

Two

The Lord made man the master. It's not up to women to try to disprove the truth," Papa had often said, and he always had the neighbors, even the minister, to turn to for sympathetic agreement.

There were few issues Lewis Bennett spoke on so strongly, as he usually was quiet and relaxed in his ways. Some guessed that his words were often spoken to convince himself. Mr. Bennett was a tall man, a straight man, even when pushing against a plow, yet he wore his tallness without authority. Within the house his wife's commands snapped the children to attention. He mouthed words of sternness, but his blue-gray eyes belied his toughness. Whether Papa recognized the fact or not, Mama quite frequently arranged to have her own will be done, and the master rarely complained.

Hannah Bennett sometimes paced with distraction because of her husband's lack of toughness and his willingness to share his neighbor's troubles.

"You've got work enough as it is, Lewis, without lending your team to the Anders. I saw a rock the size of a hog in the middle of our cornfield," she'd said one day.

"Now just how many ears of corn do you reckon would grow in that spot if I was to move that rock?" Lewis Bennett answered with a grin.

Hannah Bennett sighed, shook her head, and turned to her

19

task of scouring the kettle with a sandstone billet. "You can't always plow around your troubles, Lewis. Sometimes you have to work harder and heave them out."

"You talk as if we had a whole rock pile of troubles, Hannah." He had laughed and put his wife at ease, while she had strengthened his resolve to move that rock the following morning.

Belva's rocks weren't quite so easily moved. How could she prove she was faster than the Anders boy when she was told it was unladylike to race across the field on her way to school? There were so many things she liked to do that were forbidden. Thank goodness, book learning wasn't one of them. She loved to read.

Belva was the top student in her class at school, but this caused her little pride. Girls often did get better grades than boys.

"Why aren't there any women doctors or lawyers or mayors or presidents if women are so smart?" Belva had asked her father.

"Probably because the Lord knew it takes more brains to run a family of children who are always asking questions."

He chuckled, but Belva ran from the room before she made a "sassy answer," which always did get her into trouble. It hurt her feelings when Papa refused to take her seriously.

History was Belva's favorite subject. It was strange to think that only a few years ago Indians had hunted wild game in the fields and forests that surrounded their own stand of corn and oats. Every spring at plowing time, Papa brought home a pocketful of finely chipped arrowheads, some small and heart-shaped to pierce the soft bodies of birds, others heavy and spearlike to bring down a deer, wildcat, or bear.

Often she tried to imagine what life would have been like if she had lived during a different chapter in her history book. If she had lived a hundred years ago, she would have been governed by a king. And there had been queens, too, who had ruled centuries ago, Elizabeth of England and Cleopatra of Egypt, and now a young girl, Victoria, had been crowned queen of the whole British Empire. Not all girls sat at home stitching on their samplers and kneading a plump hand of dough, she told herself. No sense in dreaming of queens, but she guessed she'd settle at least for being a schoolteacher one day like Miss Englehardt.

Of course she'd like to have a family, too. In March, Mother had had a darling baby girl who was baptized Inverno Bennett. Belva loved to watch the tiny baby squirm and reach for the bands of sun that filtered through the windowpane, but it was Rachel who most frequently took over the care of the tiny one when Mother had to tend to Cyrene. She had been sick most of the summer with a bad cough and an ear that ached. Many nights she cried herself to sleep.

Belva knew she'd have to work hard to be a teacher like Miss Englehardt, but it was work that she loved.

Belva was only eleven years old when she had her first chance to step into Miss Englehardt's shoes. She would never forget that day. She had arrived early, as she often did, to help the teacher put slates and books on the proper desks, sometimes helping to stoke the coal stove that heated the drafty one-room shingled cottage that served as the schoolhouse.

Belva entered and hung her sweater on a hook at the back of the room and placed her lunch basket beneath that. Warren would be along later. Thirteen-year-old Rachel went to classes more or less when she felt like it. She considered school a waste of time, and Papa agreed. Only Mama kept urging her to stay on for a diploma for eighth grade, but today Mama was glad of help with the baby.

Belva turned to the bookshelf and noticed that Miss Englehardt was slumped at her desk, her head resting on her arm.

"Are you all right, Miss Englehardt?" Belva asked anxiously.

The teacher immediately straightened herself in her chair. "I'm so glad you came early, Belva. I don't know what is wrong, but I seem to be having a dizzy spell." Her usually neat auburn hair hung in damp strands around her flushed face.

"Can I get you some water from the pump?" Belva asked.

"No, thank you, but you can help, Belva. I'm going to let you take over the classes today. It is too late to cancel school, and I don't think I will be able to stay. I've already put out books and lessons. Ezra can read his paper on the pyramids. You can have a spelling bee, and the younger children might enjoy hearing a story from *Aesop's Fables.*"

Belva caught her breath. "Oh, but I couldn't be the teacher."

"Of course you can, Belva. You are the brightest one in the class. You know the lessons. It will be for only one day. I'm sure I'll be all right tomorrow."

Miss Englehardt rose from her chair unsteadily.

"Can you get home all right?" Belva asked with concern.

"I can manage if you can manage." Miss Englehardt smiled weakly. She put on her bonnet and shawl and left before Belva quite realized she was alone.

Hesitantly Belva moved to Miss Englehardt's desk. She seated herself in the straight, cane-bottom chair. Her feet barely touched the floor. Three lines of desks marched away from the blackboard in neat rows. There were eighteen places, but this year only fifteen pupils. Man-sized Ezra Zarit, called E.Z. by his peers, at sixteen was the oldest student. He would be the last to arrive because he always said he had a man-sized load of chores to finish at home. Most everyone knew that E.Z.'s early morning chore usually meant dropping a fishing line in the stream that cut across the Bennett meadow.

The youngest pupil in the school was five-year-old Toby

Taylor, who was brought to school every day by his mother because the Taylor house was crowded with two-year-old twins and a four-year-old sister. He was the first one to arrive. Mrs. Taylor didn't take time to ask where Miss Englehardt was, which pleased Belva because she wondered what parents would say if they knew the teacher for the day had reached the hardly mature age of eleven. Belva felt nervous but not frightened.

When the clock on the wall read eight, she went outside and rang the school bell. The children had assembled, but from habit no one had bothered to enter the schoolhouse until summoned. There was the usual commotion as they deposited their lunches at the back of the room and found their places. Belva took a deep breath and stepped to the front of the class.

"We will now have the pledge of allegiance to the flag."

Everyone looked around in surprise. "Where's Miss Englehardt?" asked Warren.

"She's sick today," Belva explained, "but she was here and left all our lesson assignments."

"And here I got out of bed for nothin'." It was Ezra Zarit who had spoken.

"We will have classes just as usual, E.Z.," Belva said firmly. She placed her hand over her heart and faced the flag. "I pledge allegiance . . ."

Again from habit, fourteen voices joined hers. When they finished, all the students sat down except E.Z. "I don't have to stay if we don't have a teacher," he said.

"Miss Englehardt has assigned me to be the teacher," Belva answered clearly. Her eyes stared steadily at E.Z. "We can start with your paper on the pyramids. It should be of interest to all of us."

"Now don't she just sound like a teacher?" Ezra laughed. Then slowly he added, "But she sure don't look like one."

The classroom echoed with laughter. Belva flushed. She had to pass this first test of authority. "Ezra, we'd like to hear your paper."

"I haven't finished it."

"Well then, that will give you something to do for the rest of the morning."

"I'm sure not going to mind a kid younger than me," he snorted, "and especially not a girl!"

Belva's voice remained calm. "If it isn't finished by tomorrow, I'm sure Miss Englehardt will arrange for an extra assignment, longer and harder than this one."

E.Z. hesitated, knowing Belva had spoken the truth. "Well, as long as I'm here, I might as well write a few lines, but I'm not takin' any bossin' from the likes of you."

Belva ignored the last threat. The rest of the morning went smoothly. She wrote the arithmetic problems on the blackboard for the older pupils. Verses to be memorized were assigned, and she sat with three of the younger children while they stumbled through a reading lesson. She was enjoying her day and was surprised to glance at the clock and see it was time to dismiss the class for lunch.

She waited until everyone had raced out the door before picking up her own lunch basket. E.Z. was waiting for her. She smiled a bit nervously. "Well, did you finish your paper?"

"As much as I aim to finish it. And as soon as I eat, me and the boys is takin' off. We'll leave the schoolin' for the sissy girls."

"What makes you think school is only for girls, Ezra?"

" 'Cause boys is naturally smarter and don't need to learn stupid things from books. Ever hear of a girl running a train? That's what I'm going to be in a year or two. I'm gonna work for the railroad and be an engineer."

"That's a fine idea," said Belva. "But I bet if a woman felt she wanted to, she could run a train just as well as a man. If they'd let her," she added quietly to herself.

Ezra laughed. "I ain't ever heard of a lady engineer."

The other boys began to snicker.

"I still say girls can do anything as well as boys."

"Bet you couldn't lift that rock over there." E.Z. grinned.

"That's not fair," said Belva. "I didn't say boys weren't stronger than girls, just that they weren't any smarter than girls."

"See, you're just making excuses. Watch me lift this one."

Ezra walked over to a large boulder that had been dumped in a pile where someone had started to build a stone gatepost. Rough timbers lay beside it. He strained to roll the stone over, but it was larger than he had bargained for and was half buried in the ground.

Belva watched thoughtfully for a moment. "I think I could move that stone," she said.

E.Z. slapped his knee and doubled up in laughter. "Hear it, boys. And she ain't joshin'. Why I can't even budge that hunk of stone."

"If I do move it," said Belva, "will you all promise to stay in class until the end of the day?"

"Sure, but if you don't move it, I'm gonna tell my folks teacher says I get a week off."

Belva first picked up a small stone and placed it near the bigger one. Then she chose a length of split timber about six feet long and wedged that against an undercut of the boulder. Using the smaller stone as a fulcrum for her lever, she put all her weight on the timber. The boulder slowly rolled onto its side.

E.Z.'s mouth dropped open in astonishment.

"Now if you'd read your lesson about how they built the pyramids, you would have won your challenge," said Belva.

"And that's something you may want to remember when you're a railroad man."

She went back into the schoolhouse feeling she was now an experienced teacher.

Three

A t fourteen, Belva had completed all the instruction Miss Englehardt could give her in grammar, geography, algebra, and history. On the fifth of May she would be graduating from the country school, an event she dreaded. There was so much more she wanted to learn and so much she wanted to see through books. She'd never been farther than a few miles from home, yet she studied maps to explore the country around her. The blank spaces to the west did not interest her as much as the heavy dots that pointed to the big cities.

She tried to picture in her mind what it would be like to live in a town: houses close together so there'd always be neighbors to visit; and shops, she'd heard there were stores where you could buy anything you wanted. Miss Englehardt had even told her that Buffalo had a city library housed in the new quarters of the Young Men's Association. Buffalo was no more than fifty miles, or two days' journey away. She was determined she'd get there somehow. All planning would have to start with Papa, although if Mama thought it was a good idea, the battle was won.

She'd learned not to ask right out, but during dessert at the Sunday dinner table, when the whole family was together, she said, "Papa, is it true that Buffalo has a harbor for sailing ships?"

"That it does. Ships from all over the Great Lakes."

"Are there big ships?"

"Bigger than your imagination."

"I've never seen a boat, a big boat, in my whole life," Warren added.

"It's an unforgettable sight, I'll tell you," said Papa.

"Oh please, Papa, Mama, can't we go to Buffalo sometime, please?" Belva pleaded.

Lewis Bennett looked up in surprise. "Nothing I'd better like to do, daughter, but it takes a heap of hard money to travel nowadays. There're mighty few haystacks to sleep on when you get to the city."

"We could start putting aside for it, Lewis," Mother said quietly. Belva held her breath.

"And what would you have me put aside, Hannah, the chicken eggs?" Papa smiled at his little joke.

"That's right, the chicken eggs," Mama continued, "well, some of them. And we have a side of bacon we could spare, and you yourself said the corn crop had been so good last summer that the crib was more than filled. I know for a fact that the Anders didn't plant as much as they needed last year. They'd more than likely be willing to pay you for some until the next crop comes in."

"They'd probably pay us in eggs and bacon, and then where would we be?" Lewis Bennett said.

"Now, Lewis, everyone has a wee bit of cash. Belva, get your slate and let's figure how much we'd be needing."

Belva raced upstairs and was back in a minute.

"Now let's see. How can we arrange transportation?" Mama

asked. "I don't know whether our plow horse could make it with the wagon."

"We could take the canal packet boat from Lockport," Lewis Bennett said, and then added, "that is, if we had a million dollars."

"By boat?" Belva repeated in wonder.

"We can find out from Sam Pritchett, the postmaster, how much the fare will be," Mama continued, "but we can count our other expenses right now, and I don't judge they'll quite add up to a million dollars. I talked to Sarah Reese on Sunday. She went to Buffalo last month to visit her married daughter, and she told me just what it cost her. Belva write this down. Fifteen cents a night per person for lodging, and there will be seven of us. I'd say about thirty-five cents a person for dinner, wouldn't you, Lewis?" Mama didn't wait for an answer. "We wouldn't be gone more than four or five days. Two of those nights we'd be sleeping on the canal boat."

"Who'll be doing the farm chores for four or five days?" Papa grumbled.

"I'll go see Abe Anders, Papa. I know he will without asking a cent of pay," Rachel said with enthusiasm.

"He'll do anything for you, won't he?" teased Warrie. Rachel blushed. She and Abe had been seeing each other rather frequently of late.

"That's an excellent idea," Mama agreed.

"Seems like everything has been settled without my approval," Father protested.

"Now, Lewis, that's not so at all," said Hannah Bennett. "You were the very one who suggested that we go by boat. Well, we are not arguing. We are abiding by your wishes. Now when do you think we could leave?"

Lewis Bennett shrugged his shoulders. "When the eggs have turned to gold. I wouldn't start packing just yet."

Warren rushed to the chicken coop to bring in any eggs the young hens had dropped in their nests since morning. When he returned, he had only two in his hand, but Belva wasn't disappointed. The planning had started. Besides, she didn't want to go before graduation. She was to give the valedictorian address.

It had been announced that John McNall, a village trustee of Royalton and the local inn and tavern keeper, was to give the main address before the diplomas were presented, but her talk would come first. She must be prepared. She'd hardly had time to plan what she would say, and now she couldn't think of anything except the trip to Buffalo.

During the evenings, when Mama sewed on the new lavender sprigged muslin dress she would wear for graduation, Belva jotted down fine-sounding phrases. When she put them together, they sounded empty and meaningless.

Then one night when she was struggling to get to sleep, an idea flashed across her mind. It wasn't a new thought. Mama had said it many times, but this was the right time to share it with others. The next morning she rushed to polish the words that had been whirling around in her head all night. She spent hours rehearsing the speech until she knew it perfectly.

On the fifth of May she was ready. She slipped on the pretty new outfit—for once a dress all her own. She tried to peek over Rachel's shoulder at her reflection in the mirror. There was a trace of similarity in the two faces, the point of chin, the flashing eyes, but there the sameness ended. Belva loved pretty clothes as much as her sister, but not for the same vain reason, to attract the compliments Rachel always expected. Pretty clothes made Belva feel grown up, and grownups could do so much more than children.

There were other differences that did not show in the mirror. Rachel's heart went out to a few. She could be despondent over the slightest discomfort suffered by friends or family, generously offering her solicitous help, but she could not understand Belva's concern for unfortunate strangers. Belva had almost been in tears one day after hearing a missionary from the West talk about the plight of the Navajo Indians.

"They have their own families to cry for them," Rachel had said. "They're no concern of ours."

The two sisters had had many an argument, but today there was peace. Rachel lent Belva a purple ribbon to tie in her hair, and Father had surprised everyone by stopping by the springhouse to pick a bouquet of violets for the "family's star pupil." In spite of his frequent sermons about the waste of education for young women, he admitted his pride. But there was a sting to his words.

"You're a bright girl, daughter, and I'm happy to see you've learned a heap more than your sisters or brother, but it's time to put your books away. Rachel, natural as not, will soon be setting a date for her wedding, and your mother is not as spry as she once was when it comes to butter churning and wash boiling. She'll be glad to have you home now. She'll need your help."

Belva felt both anger and helplessness. She knew this was not the time to answer her father, not until she had an answer herself. Belva pinned the violets to the sash at her tiny waist. The family lined up for final inspection. Mama smoothed Warren's stubborn hair in place one last time before they set out to walk to school.

It was a warm day. Benches had been set outside to accommodate the crowd that could hardly have squeezed into the small schoolhouse. A handmade lectern had been put together of raw lumber. A standard supported the American flag with its twenty-nine stars and thirteen stripes. The lectern had been designed for adults, and when Belva's turn came to step behind it, she found her chin instead of her elbows resting on the sloping shelf.

Someone laughed. She flushed nervously. Then she stepped to one side of the lectern and looked at the audience in front of her. Everyone she knew was there. She felt very nervous. Yet she was always asking for a chance to prove girls were capable. She could speak just as well as anyone else in class. Nothing should be different now. She caught sight of her mother's proud smile. Taking a deep breath, she started her speech.

"Dreams are the most important step toward accomplishment."

Her mother had told her that one day, and it had set Belva thinking of wonderful, preposterous plans for the future. She continued by encouraging her fellow classmates to map their own future by thinking of all the possible and seemingly impossible things they hoped might come true in their lives.

"What seems unreal today can become truth tomorrow with work, perseverance, and imagination. Would we ever have heard of Columbus or Galileo if they had failed to dream?"

The audience applauded with enthusiasm. It was the first of hundreds of speeches Belva was to give during her lifetime, but she would always remember this day. She discovered the thrill of standing before an audience. It gave her a strange feeling of power to know that many were listening to her words, that some might be influenced by them. She could not guess that she had impressed someone who was to change her own life forever.

Mr. McNall rose and turned to Belva with a smile. "Our young speaker has given a fine introduction for my own words. Just nineteen years ago a group of men saw their dreams come true. It was then that the Erie Canal, the engineering marvel of the century, was dedicated. Now we are seeing the western spread of commerce and settlement in our own community.

We must be ready for progress, for expansion. The young people of our community, of this graduating class, must be prepared."

He held the interest of his audience for almost an hour as he prophesied the changes that were still to come, "changes that seem like dreams today."

On the way home, Lewis Bennett turned to his wife. "I think I would like to see that canal, Hannah. When can we leave?"

Belva couldn't have asked for a more wonderful graduation present.

Four

One week later the family was packed and ready to go at dawn. No one wanted to take time out for more than a sampling of breakfast, but Hannah Bennett wrapped several rations of food and put them in a basket to satisfy appetites she knew were bound to develop long before they boarded the canal boat.

Papa grumbled, "We're taking enough luggage to tide us over for a year's stay."

Mama pointed out, "There are just two carpetbags. I'll not see our family disgraced in the big city because we don't know how to dress in clean Sunday best."

Lewis Bennett shook his head and hitched Maude, the work horse, to the flatbed wagon. Mama directed the piling on of five children and luggage and basket and then settled herself on the spring seat beside her husband. With a slap of leather they were off on the first leg of their journey, a two-mile ride into the village of Royalton, where they would board the stage for the ten-mile journey to Lockport.

The trip almost ended in disaster when they discovered that the stage schedule had been changed. They were either one day late or two days early, whichever way they wanted to figure. They'd planned to leave their horse and wagon with Josh Northam, who owned the general store in Royalton, but as tears flowed and anger rose, Lewis Bennett decided to turn the old wagon toward Lockport and spur Maude in a mad dash to make connections with the canal packet. It would cost more to leave the rig at a livery stable, but now that Lewis Bennett had committed himself to the trip, he threw monetary caution to the winds. "The chickens will just have to lay more," was his not-so-logical comment.

Belva was almost sick with worry that they'd miss the packet as well as the stage, but they arrived at dockside while the canal boat was still in the lower dock. This gave Lewis Bennett time to make arrangements for Maude and the family time to marvel at the huge locks, each ninety feet long, that stepped up from the deep rock gorge that had been cut at the approach to Lockport.

The canal, a forty-foot-wide highway of water that connected the Hudson River traffic from the Atlantic to the inland waters of Lake Erie, was an amazing improvement over the stage and wagon routes that were often mired in mud. Boats were now able to glide through forests and fields. Belva had even seen pictures of boats crossing hilltops where the canal stepped over valleys and rivers on man-made aqueducts. The falls at Niagara had blocked river transportation in the past. Now the 675-foot ascent to the higher level of Lake Erie was overcome by a series of 83 locks over the entire route, the most spectacular series of stairways having been constructed at Lockport, where four separate locks raised the boats a total of 60 feet. The engineering feat was now being called the Eighth Wonder of the World.

The packet was soon floated to the upper lock, and the Bennetts were able to board the *Henry Clay* to join the other passengers, most of whom had started their trip in Albany. The snub-nosed packet was built to a size, eighty by fourteen feet, to fit the locks neatly with little room to spare. Green shutters framed cottage-size windows, and folding chairs lined the top flat deck above the single cabin. The snug interior was fitted with bunks that folded against the walls fore and aft. In the center of the cabin a long table was set to serve meals to the forty passengers the boat would accommodate.

What amazed Belva most was that the boat, in spite of its load, was powered by three horses that strained at the lines secured at bow and stern. "The boat is so big. How can those poor horses ever manage to pull it?" she asked.

"Water's different than a rutted road. You'll see," Papa said. "And they'll have fresh horses to take turns all along the way."

"I'm sure glad Maude doesn't have to work like that," said Warren.

They watched as the team handler, who rode the lead horse along the towpath, urged the horses forward. The pace was slow and easy, but they had already left Lockport astern before they had settled their luggage and had been assigned their bunks for the night. Quarters for men and women would later be partitioned by a single screen.

"Papa, may we sit outside so we can see more?" Belva asked.

Lewis Bennett nodded. Warren had already found his way up the narrow stairs. It was a sunny day, and many of the passengers were already seated on the upper deck. Ladies brought out parasols, and strangers chatted so that they were strangers no more. Rachel, who usually delighted in playing the part of young lady, now clung timidly to her mother's side, frightened by the strange sights all around her. Belva's cheeks were flushed more with excitement than fear.

Just as they were seating themselves on the canvas chairs, the boatman blew his horn and called out, "Low bridge!" Suddenly a rickety structure that served as a cow path across a farmer's field loomed ahead. As they ducked to their knees, the trestle passed inches over their heads.

"Oh, Papa, do they know what they are doing? I want to get off this boat," cried Rachel.

"I believe you'll find we're not the first passengers to survive the trip," Mr. Bennett said with a laugh.

"Nor I'm sure the last," a tall fellow with sandy hair said. "May I introduce myself? I'm Uriah McNall from Royalton. I thought I recognized your family when you boarded."

Mr. Bennett shook hands warmly with the young man. "You must be John McNall's son. I knew you as a very young lad. Has it been that long? But here, let me present my own brood, Mrs. Bennett, and we have Rachel and Belva." He had started to say Warren but smiled. "You'll have to meet my son later. We can't seem to keep him in one place. And our two young ones dozing through the excitement are Cyrene and Inverno."

Uriah McNall bowed politely to each of them, then turned his attention to Belva. "I did enjoy your speech at graduation, Miss Bennett."

"You were there?" asked Belva in surprise.

"Yes. Since my father also gave a talk that day, he decided I should come along to lead the applause."

His laugh was pleasant, and when he smiled, his eyes crinkled at the corners. Belva guessed that he was four, maybe five years older than she, but this young man, fashionably dressed and traveling all the way to Buffalo alone, seemed very much a man of the world. What was he saying? She mustn't stand here tongue-tied, but Uriah McNall had already turned to Mrs. Bennett. "Will you be staying in Buffalo long?"

"Only a day or two to give the children a chance to see the city," she answered.

Belva twisted her handkerchief nervously in her lap. Now he'd think them all a passel of infants. Still he did not seem inclined to move away to talk to the other passengers. Instead, he drew up his chair to join the family group. Lewis Bennett enjoyed the opportunity to expound his views on politics, the threat of war, and the inflated cost of drilling a new well. Belva listened attentively. She was surprised that young Mr. McNall spoke so knowledgeably of President Tyler, the "common man's choice," and the new invention of Samuel Morse that made it possible to send messages over a wire.

Belva gave up hope of exchanging any words herself, but directly after dinner, which was served below, he found a seat next to hers and asked a very direct question. "Tell me, Miss Bennett, do you really believe what you said in your speech that you can make your dreams come true?"

Belva nodded thoughtfully. "If one dreams sensibly enough in the first place."

"Now do you think Columbus or Galileo were considered sensible men?"

Belva laughed. "I guess not."

"Just what are your sensible dreams?" he asked.

Belva looked up at the young man's smiling face. He really did seem interested in what she had to say, but she hesitated to answer.

"You mean you haven't started to dream?" he teased. "I can't believe it."

"No, but I haven't told a soul, and it isn't very sensible either."

"I'll keep a secret."

"I want to go on to school. There's the Girls' Academy in Royalton, but I couldn't possibly afford the tuition, and it's really foolish to think of such a thing," she blurted out in one breath.

"What about that speech you made? You'll find a way," Uriah replied encouragingly.

"If I could just earn some money myself!" Belva sighed.

"I know they are looking for a teacher for the summer months. My father told me so. Why don't you go to see him when you get back?"

"Teach school? Really teach? Do you think they would consider me?"

"Now if the decision were mine, you would be hired instantly," he said gallantly.

Belva was so excited that later she couldn't remember a thing she'd said. She wondered if she had nodded at the right time or answered any of Uriah's questions with the slightest sense. He must surely think her a scatterbrained child, not able to cope with any more education.

She spent a restless night on the narrow shelf bunk, planning what she would say to the senior Mr. McNall when she applied for the teaching job, but somehow Uriah's sandy hair and crinkle grin rated equal attention in her thoughts. Strange noises helped keep her awake—the occasional jarring of the canal boat as it nudged against the side of a lock and the creak of the strained tow rope. Home seemed a million miles away.

Early in the morning she slipped out of her bunk to the upper deck. The sun was just beginning to lighten shapes with a wash of gold before turning them back to their day colors of spring green and blossom pink. Already buildings were crowd-

37

ing together to house the thirty thousand people who lived in Buffalo. Canal traffic was heavy. Belva watched how the teamster checked his horses until the tow rope fell slack in the water so that a passing vessel could slip over the line. Boatmen sounded their horns, and already the noise of the city was upon them by the time other passengers climbed to the upper deck.

Uriah McNall was again talking to Mr. Bennett. "If you haven't been in Buffalo recently, let me recommend the Perry Inn. It's one of the best, but reasonable. I'll be staying with friends of my father."

The boat soon pulled into the terminal dock in the center of Buffalo. The masts of the lake schooners swayed like a forest in a storm. Lower to the water's edge, the rigging of fishing craft seemed tangled in a mighty thicket of stays and lines and furled sails. Warren was busy swinging his arms like a windmill. "Look here. See that over there." Rachel was strangely silent.

Mr. Bennett took charge of the luggage, and Belva helped manage the younger children as they crossed the gangplank. Uriah insisted on walking with them and carrying one of the carpetbags the three short blocks to the Perry Inn. When he left, Mr. Bennett commented to his wife, "Now there's a fine young man. Knows what's happening in this world."

"And he has manners," Mama added.

Belva thought to herself, "And such a wonderful smile."

They left their room almost immediately to explore the city. Hansom cabs, carriages, water wagons, and lumbering Conestoga rigs carrying heavy freight, helped tangle traffic. Buffalo was a city bursting with commerce, the crossroads of not only water traffic but of that new giant of transportation the railroad, serviced by the Buffalo and Attica line. Papa marveled how the city had grown since he'd last seen it. Most of the buildings had been hastily constructed, but there was an air of pretension as if to prove their permanence. Porticos, columns, domes, and colonades had been added, all in raw wood that had not yet achieved the mellow weathering of age.

Hannah Bennett and the girls wanted to look at, if not to purchase, the latest fashions displayed by pictures in the windows of dozens of shops that lined the board walks. Papa finally hit upon the solution that Mama could not possibly get lost in a bonnet shop while he and Warren took a look at the printing press of the *Commercial*, the city newspaper, copies of which occasionally found their way to Royalton.

"You look at your geegaws to your heart's content, and we'll be back to find a place to eat within the hour."

For three days Belva marveled at the wonders of a modern city. She had her wish to visit the city library and couldn't believe there were that many books in the whole world. She made a firm commitment with herself. She was going to see the rest of the world, at least as much of it as she could manage.

Five

To help make that dream come true, she'd have to earn her own money, and to secure a job, she'd have to have more education, and to pay for her schooling, she'd have to find work. Circles always seemed to close around her. It was a week after their return before Belva could make an excuse to go to Royalton. She must return some books that belonged to Miss Engle-hardt. It was a half truth, but she'd not risk talking to Mama or Papa about her job plan for fear they'd forbid it.

She practiced pinning up her braids to add years to her appearance. It was too bad she didn't wear glasses, she thought, but she dressed with care and borrowed Mama's crocheted shawl. By the time she'd reached the outskirts of Royalton, where the country road was edged with neat garden fences, she'd almost changed her mind. Surely there must be others better qualified for the teaching job.

She might have abandoned her plan if she hadn't met Mr. John McNall in front of the general store. Mr. McNall tipped his hat and was the first to speak. "Did you enjoy your trip to Buffalo, Miss Bennett? I heard from Uriah that you and your family had an excursion on our great Erie Canal. How did you like it?"

Belva at once felt at ease. "I think I have you to thank for the trip, Mr. McNall," she said. "Your talk at graduation interested Father so much that he wanted to see the canal for himself."

He laughed. "I'm glad I impressed someone." His voice reminded her of Uriah's. Only his full beard masked the amazing likeness of features he shared with his son. He was about to enter the store, and Belva knew she must ask the important question now.

"Mr. McNall, is it true that you are looking for a teacher for the district school this summer?"

Mr. McNall looked at her quizzically and nodded.

"I would like to apply for that job. I have completed all the basic courses under Miss Englehardt, and I . . . ."

"Hold on there a minute, Miss Bennett. Just how old are you?"

Belva hesitated; then tilting her chin, she answered firmly.

"Fourteen, sir. I have completed all eight years of grammar school."

"And do you think you could manage those husky farm lads who have an edge on you in years and size?"

"Yes, Mr. McNall. I'm sure I can. I can manage my brother with no trouble at all." He laughed. "And I do believe with the extra reading I have been doing that I could direct a full curriculum of study."

Mr. McNall's smile turned to a thoughtful frown. Belva clenched her fists at her sides. If wishing hard enough could bring the right answer, she'd have no trouble at all. "Say yes, say yes," kept going through her mind.

After a long hesitation he answered, "You can have the job on a trial basis, Miss Bennett. Seven dollars a week is all it pays, but if you . . ."

"That is most satisfactory, Mr. McNall," Belva answered quickly. One step had been taken to break the circle, that is, if Papa would give his permission.

As expected, Papa was dead set against her leaving. "There's plenty of work around here for you to do. Your mother needs help."

Mama interrupted. "You keep referring to me as if I were an invalid. Have I really aged that much, Lewis? Perhaps I should start dyeing my hair the way I heard talk some actresses in Buffalo are doing."

"Now don't you go getting any silly ideas. One in the family . . ."

"Has your home ever been neglected? Has the cooking suffered?"

"No. No of course not," Papa answered.

"Well then, I don't need Belva around to give me help, not yet in life I don't."

Mr. Bennett knew better than to argue further. Belva took

41

over the summer job and proved that she not only could manage the older students but teach them a great deal as well. Their final tests proved it.

At the end of the summer Belva counted her savings and judged that she would have enough for her tuition at the Girls' Academy and a meager allotment for living expenses. She had arranged to earn most of her board by keeping house for an elderly widow, Mrs. Pryor, who lived near the school.

She was moving only a few miles from the Bennett farm, but this was her first move toward real independence. Her future was hers to plan, and she had an insatiable curiosity to find out what the world was like beyond Niagara County.

As she said good-bye, Mama squeezed her hand tightly. "I envy you, my dear," she said.

Papa shook his head. "You'll just be disappointed with your lot when you come back, too full of books to bake a biscuit."

"Why, Papa, she'll be able to write a book telling womenfolk how to bake their biscuits," Warrie teased.

Belva smiled, but she wished the farewells were over. She was anxious to start, anxious and, yes, a bit nervous.

At first Belva was disappointed with her new surroundings. The other girls at the academy seemed strange to her. Most of them had come from larger communities, a few even from Buffalo. Surely those who came so far at a time when parents rarely thought it necessary to provide further education for their daughters came from backgrounds far more affluent than the Bennetts'. Yet perhaps because of this, because responsibility had rarely come their way, Belva's classmates seemed childishly immature to her.

Many of the girls were homesick. They disliked the regimentation of school. Studying was frequently a bore. Their free time was spent chattering about girl matters, clothes and boys, boys and clothes. Belva rarely joined them for social hours as she was expected back at Mrs. Pryor's when classes were over.

However, Belva did have a regular gentleman caller herself, Uriah McNall. When he first arrived at Mrs. Pryor's front door, Belva was delightfully surprised. It had been five months since they had met on the trip to Buffalo. He was as handsome as she had remembered, standing before her dressed in the latest fashion, a brocade vest showing beneath his broadcloth jacket. He was clean-shaven, but he had left his sideburns curly to compliment his rather thin face. His eyes smiled, and he at once made apologies for not having called sooner.

"I'm working for a lumber mill not far from here in Gasport, but it was not until this very day that I learned from my father that the bright young schoolteacher he had hired for the summer had now returned to school herself. You did make that dream come true."

"I guess it was sensible after all." She laughed. "Please won't you come in for a cup of tea?"

They sat in Mrs. Pryor's company parlor exchanging pleasantries about the lack of rain for the garden roses. Belva's calm poise seemed to vanish. Words refused to come to her mind, and her face flushed so that she was sure he sensed her uneasiness. Young Mr. McNall, however, was really not such a man of the world that he was used to a brilliant young lady conversationalist. Belva had but to ask him how he enjoyed his new job, and her role as listener was well established. His enthusiasm took over.

"The opportunities are tremendous. There is a chance that I may be able to buy an interest in the sawmill. Eventually I'd like to get into the building field myself. Others are putting up stores and homes on speculation so that new settlers do not have to wait to bring their families to western New York. Of

43

course I must save the money first, and that does seem to take a bit of doing." His serious frown gave way to a grin.

"It sounds like an excellent idea, Mr. McNall," said Belva. "Perhaps a loan could be arranged at a bank on small interest for such a worthwhile project that would bring growth to the community."

Uriah seemed startled. Then he threw back his head and laughed.

Belva flushed. "I did not mean to be presumptuous, Mr. Mc-Nall."

"Presumptuous? I should say not. I apologize for my laughter. Those are the very words that my father used, but I did not expect them to be repeated by such an unexpected source. And where did you ever learn about banking, Miss Bennett?"

"Only from hearsay and from books, but it would seem only logical that the community would gain from such an enterprise and that there would be others who would be delighted to see your venture prosper."

"For the first time you have given me confidence. 'Dream so as not to limit accomplishment.' Weren't those your words? I intend to apply for that loan tomorrow. I may yet own my own business before you graduate, Miss Bennett."

Uriah continued to build his dreams, but there were many disappointments, which he discussed with Belva. The owner of the sawmill would not sell an interest in his profitable business, and he had insured himself against competition by leasing most of the timberland within a practical radius of Royalton, Gasport, and Lockport. Commerce and trade in the area were being generated by the westward flow of immigrants from the eastern seaboard, but men with ready capital from the East were reaping the rewards.

Uriah's savings grew very slowly. He kept his steady job at the sawmill and continued to search for backers of his building schemes. Some of his salary was spent on "dandy clothes," as he called them, to impress prospective investors he met on his frequent trips to Buffalo. Disappointment did not seem to dampen his enthusiasm for the future, and Belva herself agreed with his logic that with more and more people moving into the area, opportunity was bound to come his way.

As the months rolled on, Uriah frequently used the word "we" in his plans for the future. By the time Belva was ready to graduate in her eighteenth year, he had proposed marriage. Belva had long ago decided to accept, but before any formal announcement was made, Uriah called on Mr. and Mrs. Bennett. Again he outlined his glowing plans for the future, minimizing the small salary he earned at the sawmill. The Bennetts were well pleased. Rachel had already married her beau, Abe Anders, and John Bennett had been secretly worried that Belva's schooling might have turned her into an old maid, a distressing position in those days.

"I'm glad to see you settling down as was intended," Papa said.

"I liked him from the first," Mama added.

A simple wedding was planned with only a few of the neighbors present. Rachel stood beside her sister at the altar of the country church. Papa was nervous. Mama smiled, but Warren seemed to take his sister's marriage hardest of all. "You've gotta promise to come back for Christmas," he said.

"I'll not be more than an hour away," Belva assured him.

Mama carefully packed an heirloom teapot, one of her prized possessions, in the bottom of Belva's little chest that had been accumulating linens and quilts from the time Belva put away her rag dolls. Again she said good-bye to her family. Belva and Uriah boarded a borrowed wagon and headed for their new home and a new adventure.

Six

The community of Gasport was considerably larger than Royalton, but most buildings carried the rawness of new timber. Only a few roads had been planked to cover spring mud. Storefronts had been hastily constructed on whatever level and style was their owner's whim. The wooden sidewalk that meandered down the main street of town stepped up and down to meet the varying levels of the doorjambs. It was not the fine new city plan Uriah had described, but Belva sensed his pride and enthusiasm for the town.

As they passed, he pointed out the new livery stable and stage shop that was still under construction. "I delivered five loads of fine pine last week, and they're asking for more."

At the farthest end of town he pulled the wagon into a rutted path that led to a small planked cottage. The sloping eaves of the house almost touched the ground on two sides, like the wings of a mother hen settled over her nest. A split-rail fence bordered an untended garden. Although the gate was broken, a rosebush welcomed them by the front door. Again Belva was surprised that the house did not match Uriah's description, but she remembered he had been putting aside what he could to start his own business. Surely this sensible economy was an admirable trait for a young husband.

Belva had no trouble finding admirable traits for her bridegroom. He had a warm sense of humor, and no problem was too serious to dampen his spirits. His curiosity matched her own. Frequently they talked of making the trip to Washington someday. And, what was most important to Belva, Uriah shared his discussions of current events and business with her. At first he seemed amused that she would have serious comments of her own, but he was soon consulting her on politics and on money matters, the latter a subject on which, if fault were to be found, he was none too practical.

Belva at once set about making the little cottage into a cheerful and comfortable home. The teapot was placed on a shelf above the hearth. The green and yellow quilt was tucked over the featherbed on its rope frame in the corner. The wooden floor, the only renovation Uriah had provided for his bachelor quarters, had been sanded and scrubbed to a hint of luster. The shed at the back could be made into an extra room someday, and then she'd have quarters almost as spacious as the Bennett homestead.

Uriah began to talk of much bigger plans. If he built a luxurious home for himself, he predicted others would come to look at it and order similar ones for their own families. All he needed was the money to hire a carpenter and helper. The lumber he could have on credit.

But Belva guessed that this first cottage would hold their fondest memories. The house was in sight of the mill, which made it possible for Uriah to come home for midday dinner, instead of having to carry his meal in a pail as most men did. She remembered the first day watching impatiently for him, unable to concentrate on a single word in the book she held in her hands. When she recognized his familiar stride as he came down the path, she threw her book to the floor and hurried to the door. She turned for a moment, imagining her mother's scolding tone: "Put things away, Belva. A tidy house means a tidy mind."

Then she laughed. "But this is my house. I can do as I please."

She skipped past the door and ran down the path. Uriah smiled at his wife, who one moment could appear a most dignified young matron and the next a tomboy who could climb apple trees or rooftops. She had told him the story. Had it happened only ten years ago?

He matched her mood of reckless abandon and caught her lightly around the waist and swung her high in a dizzy circle.

When Uriah could spare the time, they packed picnics and climbed the wooded hills to a spot where the village was spread at their feet like a tumble of toy buildings. Once a rainstorm caught them unaware, and they'd raced for home, Belva almost winning.

"If I hadn't worn your coat, I would have crossed the door first," she teased.

"And just why do you think I was so gallant?" he said.

Belva enjoyed the evenings the most. They'd sit by the fire talking of buiness matters and world affairs. Uriah subscribed to the *United States Magazine and Review*. Rachel would have died of boredom, but for Belva this was a close substitute for travel, which she still dreamed of.

"I cannot understand how President Polk could sign such an unjust treaty with Mexico. He is stealing their land," Uriah said.

"I agree that the terms were harsh, but the United States has paid for the land," Belva argued.

"A pittance we've paid, and just at a time when we're rolling in wealth. With the gold they're finding in California, our country will soon be the richest nation in the world."

"You would be heading west right now if we weren't married, wouldn't you, Uriah?" Belva asked with concern.

"I'm a lot surer of making my fortune here, and I'm a heap

more comfortable sitting in my rocking chair than braving a scalping party a thousand miles from home." He laughed. "I'm either cowardly or lazy or both."

"I won't let you say things like that, even in jest," said Belva.

Suddenly he turned serious. "The West is no place to raise a family, and besides I'd miss these green hills."

Belva believed him and was content. Uriah's plans for the future did seem to be taking shape. The lumber business was booming. Prices continued to soar as supply never seemed to catch up with demand. He was sent to Lockport to contract for a sizable order of lumber, enough for a new hotel and a church. He would share a commission on the order, enough so that they might reasonably expect to start their own home. Uriah hoped to draw up the plans during the winter when he'd have time to spare.

For almost a year nothing spoiled their happiness, but when tragedy did strike, it was a terrifying blow. Belva had gone out to the chicken yard one morning to search for the hen's eggs. She hadn't noticed that the whine of the saw blades at the mill had stopped. Only when she looked up and saw a horse and rider cutting across the field in her direction did a hint of fear tighten her throat. She shaded her eyes to see who it was. Jonathan Muste, the foreman at the mill, was riding fast. He reined his horse to a sudden halt at the garden fence. A chill struck Belva's heart. She ran toward him.

"There's been an accident, Mrs. McNall."

Belva didn't wait to hear more. She tore open the gate and started running toward the mill.

"Stay here, Mrs. McNall. They're bringing him in a wagon. I'm going to get the doctor now."

Still Belva didn't stop. She ran on to meet the wagon that she could see slowly cutting across the field. What a short distance it had seemed before! Now her stumbling steps took forever to meet the wagon. The driver helped her climb aboard. Uriah's still body was cushioned on a pile of rough burlap sacks. His face was white. His breathing came in gasps. A thin line of blood trickled from the corner of his mouth. Gently she wiped it away with her apron.

"What happened?" It didn't sound like her voice that had asked.

"A load of logs let loose from the main stack. One struck and pinned against his chest," the driver answered.

She fought back hysterical tears. She must be calm or she'd be no help at all. "There's an old door by the woodshed we can use as a stretcher." She held Uriah's hand, but it felt cold and lifeless. She shuddered.

By the time they reached the gate, Jonathan Muste had returned with the doctor. Gently they lowered Uriah's limp body on the makeshift stretcher and carried him into the house. They eased him unto the bed.

Already the young doctor was loosening Uriah's clothing and gently feeling for broken bones.

"Will he be all right?" Belva asked, almost afraid to hear the answer.

It was some time before the doctor replied. "Not much any of us can do now. I can splint his arm, but what's broken inside only the Lord can heal."

For two days Uriah remained unconscious. Word had reached the Bennetts of the accident. Belva's mother came at once, but there was little they could do. Neighbors dropped by with dishes of hot food. Belva had no appetite.

"It is not right to pray to the Lord for help if you do not help yourself," Hannah Bennett warned sternly. "Food will give you strength."

Belva forced herself to try some stew, but she would not leave her husband's side. When Uriah opened his eyes, Belva buried her head against his pillow and sobbed hysterically. She was later to write that it was the first and the last time in her life that she ever lost complete control of her emotions. When at last she composed herself, the tears had washed away the anxiety that drained her of energy. Now she was sure that he would recover. She must keep herself well to nurse him back to health.

Slowly, very slowly, his body began to heal. The splints were removed from his arm, but he tired easily and often slept till noon. He spent much of the time staring silently at the walls around him. It was as if his spirit had been crushed by the load of logs. Belva tried to cheer him. She read to him frequently, but he rarely made a comment. She tried to talk to him of the fine plans for their new home, although in her heart she was afraid these plans must be put away forever.

Uriah took little notice of the fact that now Belva had an extra load on her shoulders. Although the cottage was small and there were only a few acres of land to tend, there was still the milk cow, the chickens, and the sow with her piglets to care for. Corn for the animals had to be stacked, the strawberry plants bedded, and it was now time to fill the root cellar under the toolshed with carrots and onions and squash that would last through the winter. Mother had stayed only a few days, but Warren, now a strong young man, came every week to help with the heavier chores, such as fixing the roof on the chicken house and butchering the pork.

Three months passed before Uriah opened the front door on the world around him. With Belva's help he made his way to a chair in the garden. Frost had already withered the once scarlet leaves, and the wind whipped them in rustling swirls against the fence. Uriah sat bundled in a shawl and blanket looking down the valley toward the mill.

"I feel so useless," he said.

Belva put her hand on his frail arm. "But you are gaining strength, I can tell." She hesitated. "Perhaps if you talked to Mr. Muste, there would be a part-time job that would keep you occupied."

He nodded. "You are right. I've been a burden long enough."

"Uriah, that is not what I mean. There is no hurry for you to return to the mill. We are not hungry. I was only thinking it would do you good to get out and see people."

"Today is as good a time as any to ask if they will have me," he added.

"I'll get my shawl and go with you," said Belva. "You shouldn't walk so far alone until you are stronger."

Together they made their way up the path to the mill. Once Uriah stopped to catch his breath, but he wouldn't listen to Belva's suggestion that they turn back and wait for another day. Jonathan Muste greeted them with surpirse and pleasure. "Glad to see you up and about, Uriah."

"Do you have work for a cripple like me?" Uriah asked with a wry smile.

"Your job is always open for you," Muste answered, "when you feel up to it."

"I'll be back tomorrow. Thank you."

From that morning on Uriah did not miss a day of work, but he often returned home exhausted, too tired even to eat his evening meal. It was a lonely time for Belva and one of fear that Uriah would never recover his energy and spirit. They did not want for food and shelter, but somehow their little cottage seemed drab and ugly to her now. When the wind blew from the north, fine buff-colored trails drifted from the peaks of sawdust at the mill to her windowsill, and the whine of the saw rasped against her nerves.

Still their life together began to take on a more normal pattern. A year after the accident Belva knew that she was going to have a baby. Uriah at once began to take new interest in life. The future was suddenly important now. He brought out the old plans for their house and showed Belva where they could put the baby's cradle and how they could arrange the family rooms.

"If it's a girl, you must promise to keep her from climbing apple trees, at least for a while." For the first time in a year Belva heard her husband laugh.

They named their daughter Lura. She was a pretty baby. Even the neighbors said so. Belva wished her mother could see her new granddaughter, but Hannah Bennett was home, busy taking care of Rachel's two young ones, and Rachel was about to give birth to another. Mrs. Bennett sent a tiny knit sweater and words of love, adding that she hoped Belva and her family could come home for a visit soon.

Somehow the time had never been right, what with Uriah's illness and her own confinement, and Belva rarely felt a desire to return home as long as Warren came every so often to bring word of Mama and Papa. She loved her family, but she was happy with her independence. Besides, she was constantly busy with Lura, who seemed remarkably active, toddling from chair to door to garden gate a good month before her first birthday.

Uriah continually bragged about the precocious child. At two she could recite short verses. She shared her parents' curiosity for the world around her. Her horizon might be bounded by the meadow fence, but it was full of adventure. Belva often watched her husband and daughter walk through the fields hand in hand in search of a rabbit's hole or a fox's trail. In the evening Uriah never tired of sitting beside the hearth, Lura on his knee, spinning tales of fantasy that made dreams of joy. Life was as it should be.

Then one day Uriah came home early from the mill. His face was flushed, and he complained of pains in his chest. By evening his fever had increased. Belva tucked Lura in her crib and went to summon the doctor.

Doctor Mosley tried the only treatment he knew, drawing off blood to purify his patient's system. Uriah's remaining strength ebbed, and during the night he died quietly in his sleep. The funeral took place the next day. Only the minister's wife and two neighbors were there to comfort her.

She could not realize that Uriah was gone. At the time of the accident she had prepared herself for the worst, but now shock numbed her senses. What would she do, a widow at twenty-two with a child to support?

PART II

"Words Give Us Power"

Seven

One week after the funeral Belva left little Lura at her neighbor's house for a few hours. Dressed carefully in her widow's black, she presented her credentials to the district supervisor of schools. She had a letter of recommendation from her summer teaching job and her prized diploma from the academy. He was most courteous and confirmed the fact that, yes, there was an opening for a teacher of literature and history for advanced pupils.

"We will be most happy to hire you, Mrs. McNall. I had been hoping to employ a man who perhaps could demand more respect from the older students, but we have not found one with your qualifications and experience. You may start to work this fall."

"Thank you," said Belva. "May I ask what salary I will receive?"

The supervisor hesitated for a moment. "I believe eight dollars a week is sufficient."

Belva was surprised, disappointed, and angry. She would never be able to support herself and Lura on those wages. "And what salary would you give to a male teacher?" she asked.

"The starting salary is usually between sixteen and twenty dollars a week."

"And would my duties be the same as that of a man?"

The supervisor moved uncomfortably in his chair. "Why yes, Mrs. McNall, but I do not see why that should be an issue."

"I believe that it is. I would work as hard as he. I would be responsible for the same number of students. I would expect the same payment."

"That is impossible, Mrs. McNall," he answered. "If you want the position at eight dollars a week, it is yours. If not, we will look further."

"Thank you, sir," said Belva, "but I do not think I could be satisfied unless I were judged on my own ability as a teacher, irrespective of my sex. I am sorry I have taken your time."

She left the office abruptly. Her face was flushed with anger at the unfairness of his offer. She wished she could talk to someone about her problem. Then she remembered the wife of the Methodist minister who had been so kind at the time of Uriah's accident and after his death. She had urged Belva to call on her at any time.

On impulse Belva hurried down the tree-lined street to the parsonage. Mrs. Leland greeted her warmly.

"I'm so glad you dropped by, my dear." Then she noticed Belva's agitation. "Is there something wrong? Please come in."

Belva sat on the edge of her chair as she told of her interview. "It is so unfair. I was hoping you might speak to some of the trustees, presenting my credentials and assuring them that I am a conscientious person who would never shirk my duties."

"I am sorry, Mrs. McNall. I'm sure they know that, but their salary offer will be the same. There is really nothing I can do to help. Your only fault is that you are a woman, and that is the way of the world."

"Then I will do everything in my power to change those ways. If only the world would just give us a chance to prove ourselves! Perhaps if I prepare myself with further education, attending a college, they would respect my qualifications."

Mrs. Leland shook her head sadly. "I admire your determination, but you will always have to fight prejudice."

Belva returned to her home and to Lura. Had she been rash in turning down the teaching job? How would she support herself? The words of the minister's wife burned deep into her mind. How could she fight that prejudice? She'd spoken of going on to college, but how could she afford such a luxury, and who would take care of Lura?

Answers came slowly to her mind. She could finance her education by selling the property Uriah owned in Gasport. There would be little left after debts were paid, but if she managed carefully, there would be enough for tuition and meager living expenses for perhaps two years. She'd write to her mother and ask if she'd agree to bring up little Lura while she was away at college. But what college would accept women? She'd make inquiries.

She took out her writing pad and composed two letters, the first to her mother, the second to Genesee Wesleyan Seminary, which was later to be known as Syracuse University.

Mama's answer was delivered by Warren. "I am delighted you have decided to return to school. No one can degrade the value of education. More women should have this opportunity. And as for Lura, she will help brighten our lives. However, I must tell you of our own plans. We are moving to Illinois. We will be renting a few acres and a house. Your father will be managing the adjoining farm. Things have not been going as well as they should, and your father feels that our future lies there. Although there will be more miles that separate us, our thoughts and our prayers will be with you as always."

Illinois? How could she send her little daughter so far away? And what of her mother's remark that things had not been going so well for the Bennett family? She must not be an extra burden to them. First, she must manage her own affairs. The letter of acceptance from Genesee arrived. She then decided to go ahead with her plans to sell Uriah's property in Gasport. His father offered to take care of settling the small estate for her. Despite his help, however, she ran into almost unbelievable problems, but once it was done, she packed her possessions into her leather-strapped trunk. Mama and Papa were not leaving until the end of the summer, so she decided to go back to Royalton to see them before they left, no matter what her own decisions for the future would be. She had little other than Lura's clothing and her own and the teapot. The rest of her things she sold or gave to neighbors.

When Warren came to pick them up in the wagon, Belva at once began to question him about family affairs.

"Papa will never be satisfied until he follows the rainbow west," Warren explained. "Jeremiah Gruber, who owned the farm bordering the south section of ours, packed up and left a year ago. He came back this spring to settle some accounts, and he talked Pa into joining him in Illinois. As it is, Pa hasn't even bothered to plant a crop worth mentioning this summer, and Ma is worried. Having Lura with her will take her mind off a lot of things she shouldn't be fretting over. It's just that this is the first time she hasn't been able to talk Pa out of a 'stubborn' decision, as she puts it."

Belva expected to find the family in a turmoil, but when she arrived, everything seemed to be as usual. Both Mama and Papa greeted them warmly. Of course Papa was not without a lecture about her plans for school. Yet his stern manner was lightened with humor.

"And what would happen to this world if women gave up raising families and caring for the home? Civilization would come to an end, and the Lord would have to decide whether it was worth the effort to start all over again. Surely he'd have to improve on Eve." He chuckled.

Belva was more concerned when Rachel criticized her. "It is unseemly for a married woman to go traipsing off to college, and at your age. There will be talk that you've lost your mind."

"I'm not losing it, Rachel, just trying to fill it with knowledge that can help me live a satisfying life, able to bring up my daughter in an atmosphere of tolerance."

"It's humiliating to have you talk like this." Rachel stomped out of the room. The two sisters rarely saw each other after that.

Belva's mother was the one who finally brought the argument to a close. "Now don't you worry about a thing. Lura will be in good hands, and Lewis assures me that the winters are milder in Illinois and that we will be living in luxury in no time."

There was a hint of sarcasm in her voice, but Lewis Bennett put his arm around his wife's shoulder and looked her seriously in the eyes. "I promise you I will be a good provider, Hannah. This will be our dream together."

Hannah Bennett's smile testified love and agreement. She pressed his hand with hers and turned away so that no one could see the tears in her eyes. "I know you will, Lewis. I know it."

The decision was made. Lura seemed delighted with the idea that she was going on a trip with Grandma and Grandpa. It was Belva's eyes that filled with tears this time.

Belva later wrote that "after much mending and turning of a scanty wardrobe, I again packed my trunk and made the sixty-mile journey to Lima, New York." She enrolled at Genesee Wesleyan and paid her $8.50 tuition charge for the first semester. Her curiosity urged her to take on entirely new fields of interest. She followed the "scientific course," studying such modern subjects as magnetism, electro-chemistry, mathematics pure and mixed, political economy, and the Constitution of the United States.

All students were required to furnish their own lights, pails, wash bowls, towels, and mirrors, and the lady students were charged $1.25 extra a term for the "sawing and carrying of wood."

It was the year 1854. Belva was caught up in an air of excitement. Here were other people who were asking questions of the future, others of intellectual curiosity. During the middle of the nineteenth century, any young woman who enrolled in college most assuredly had proved herself outstanding in scholarship and serious intent and would be able to find a new place for herself in the rapidly changing world. It was a time of reform, a time of commitment, and Belva found many causes with which she could identify.

The abolitionists were urging legislation to punish the slave states. Temperance societies were fighting for laws to end the sale of liquor. The platform of the Free Soilers was "free soil, free speech, free labor, free men." And there were those who believed in Belva's pet issue that women should have equal rights. She and her classmates discussed the declaration of rights drawn up eight years before at the Seneca Falls convention by the rebel reformers, Elizabeth Cady Stanton and Lucretia Mott.

Groups of young women at the college gathered for their own debates. Belva often found herself the leader of such groups. She was older than her fellow students, who had not interrupted their schooling for marriage, family, and widowhood, and she had already experienced the unfairness of prejudice against women in seeking a job. She found that she could readily express herself before the public on this issue of equal rights in which she so fervently believed. However, some of her friends were more conservative. They felt that perhaps it was suitable for the Quakers among them to speak privately of their equal rights theory, but to take the platform in their own defense, to make spectacles of themselves in public, was unseemly, unladylike.

All agreed, however, that the laws of the land were unfair. Married women had no right to own property, even if it was their own inheritance. If they were deserted by their husbands and had to earn their living, they had no title to these earnings. Women were considered inferior to men, unable to manage their affairs.

One day she read a notice posted on the bulletin board announcing that Miss Susan B. Anthony would be giving a lecture in the school auditorium the following week. Belva was anxious to attend. Perhaps she would be able to find out what others were doing to promote women's rights. Belva arrived early to be sure that she would find a seat in the crowded hall. Miss Anthony's words had been quoted in some of the editorial pages of the country's newspapers. Already she was a figure of controversy, and her enemies, as well as sympathizers, had come to hear her words.

When she appeared on the platform, Belva was surprised at her appearance. Here was no militant exhibitionist. Susan B. Anthony was dressed in the quiet fashion of a Quaker, a severely plain gray dress and hat, a picture of modest sobriety. Yet her earnest words dramatically called her listeners to task for letting such injustice exist.

While other reformers were used to going off on tangents to fight for the causes of abolition and temperance and pacifism, Miss Anthony limited her speech to two main issues, advocating changes in property rights for women and granting women the right to vote. Women's suffrage was not a new issue, but the thought that it would be taken seriously by any but the most radical reformers was certainly a change. A few prominent men, a very few, had permitted their names to be used as sponsors for this meeting where universal suffrage was discussed, but not one had been known to support such legislation.

"Women themselves must lay the question of women's wrongs before the public," said Susan B. Anthony, "for women alone can understand the height, the depth, the length, and the breadth of their degradation."

The color rose in Belva's face. She applauded. There must be something she could do to help this remarkable woman.

Miss Anthony continued. "If we stand together in our demands for recognition, we will win our battle, but our two enemies are public apathy and the power of man to beguile woman into accepting her inferior position."

When the meeting was over, Belva went back to her room and wrote a letter to her mother, telling her of the lecture and repeating some of Susan B. Anthony's inspiring words. Mama would understand.

There were times when Belva longed to sit down and talk with her mother, and there was never a day that she did not pray that Lura was safe and happy. She was always impatiently waiting for the mail to bring her news of her family so far away. Mama's first letters were cheerful and hopeful for the future. The only minor cloud to their happiness seemed to be Cyrene's illness, but Belva did not worry. Cyrene had suffered spells of poor health before.

Then a letter arrived stating the news. "Last night Cyrene died in her sleep. She had had a high fever which the doctor had not been able to control, but the end came as a shock to us all."

Belva could not believe it. Cyrene was four years younger than she was, just twenty. She had so much living yet ahead of her. In the same letter a large piece of paper had been folded and refolded many times. On it was drawn a house with a chimney billowing scallops of smoke. A bright tree with a winged spot of color arched over the top of the page. The bottom was signed in large letters LURA. Belva tacked the picture to the wall of her room. It was a cheerful picture, but tears filled her eyes, tears of grief for her sister and of loneliness about being so far from Lura.

Summer meant vacation for many, but Belva planned to stay on so she could complete her course of study in record time. Besides, she did not have the money needed for the trip to Illinois. She had to be very frugal until she was sure that her education would be able to pay for her own and her daughter's future.

The summer seemed very long. She had set herself a heavy reading schedule that she was barely able to finish before the fall term began in September. Belva was busier than ever, and now at last the months seemed to rush by until Christmas broke her class schedule. As the other students left for home, Belva stayed on to work on her thesis so that there would be no question of her graduating the following June. A two-year course was all that was offered.

Carefully she saved her package from home to be opened Christmas morning. She pictured the family gathered around the tree singing carols, although this year there would only be Mama and Papa, sister Inverno, and Lura. Rachel and her family and Warren were still living in New York State. For a moment she thought she would break down in tears. Instead, she forced herself to consider the reasons she had chosen this temporary loneliness. She was fighting for the right to earn her living honestly without charity and with independence.

She bundled herself in her new shawl and mittens and walked briskly through the town until the street became a snow-covered path rutted by wagon and sleigh. The cold wind helped clear her mind. She would soon find a teaching job and settle down with Lura. She would be able to teach her daughter and her pupils that the world need not suffer from prejudice and intolerance. Men and women of different color and beliefs ought to share equally in the privileges of citizenship. If she could influence only one person to follow this creed, her work would be worthwhile.

Drifts had already filled the path, but she plodded on unmindful of the fact that her boots were thick with ice and the hem of her coat and dress frozen in stiff folds. When she returned to her room, she fixed herself a pot of tea and then burrowed under the covers. Another night came to her mind, the night Sammy had had her kittens.

Just before graduation in June of 1857, Dr. Joseph Cummings, president of the college, asked Belva to come to see him. She was surprised and a little nervous. When she entered his office, he rose and greeted her warmly.

"Mrs. McNall, we are very pleased with your work and would like to offer you the position of preceptress of the Lockport Union School District. Before you give me your answer, I'd like to explain what your duties would be. A short time ago there were seven small schools in Lockport, each organized separately, each following a very different curriculum of study. However, Mr. Sullivan Cavernot, president of the Board of Education, has recently consolidated the school system. New buildings have been built, and they are looking for an administrator who can improve the academic standards of the young people of the town. You would be responsible for the education of some six hundred boys and girls between the ages of fourteen and eighteen. This is perhaps a more demanding job than my own as college president, but it is a challenging opportunity."

Belva was overwhelmed. She had assumed that after graduation she would have no problem finding a teaching job, but the fact that she had been offered such responsibility frightened her.

"I don't know whether I am qualified for such a project, sir," she said timidly.

Dr. Cummings smiled. "That doesn't sound like you at all, Mrs. McNall, having heard your last lecture on the rights of women to shoulder responsibility outside the home." Then with mock acceptance he frowned. "Of course we have other applicants under consideration. We could . . ."

Belva interrupted quickly. "I would be honored to accept the position, Dr. Cummings. I will do the very best I can."

He rose to shake her hand. "You know that you can always come to us with your problems, Mrs. McNall, and you will have many in this position."

"I will try very hard to solve them, sir," Belva answered.

"I'm sure that you will, Mrs. McNall, but remember that not everyone will approve of your solutions."

Eight

With the security of a job for the coming year, Belva felt able to dip into her meager savings for the journey to Illinois to visit with her family and to bring Lura back with her. She changed trains in Chicago for the short trip downstate.

Papa, Mama, Inverno, and Lura were at the station to greet her. Mama had a few more gray hairs. Papa had put on a bit of weight. Sister Inverno was a striking young lady of sixteen, but Belva's eyes lingered on her precious curly-headed daughter, who rushed into her arms.

"She did remember me," Belva whispered to herself. A great fear was lifted from her mind.

Belva had only a few days' visit with her parents. There was so much to do before school started, meeting the teaching staff, discussing curriculum, finding a place to live, but the family was well and happy, it seemed. The loss of Cyrene had been tragic, but after more than a year they had come to accept it. They were still renting land, but Papa, with his eternal optimism, felt that next year's crops would bring them a profitable share.

Mama was delighted to hear all the news from Belva, not only about her classes, but about the people Belva had met at the lectures she so often attended.

"I'm glad at least one in our family has had a chance for an education, not that Rachel and Warren aren't happy in their chosen life. Some are meant for school and some aren't, I expect. I just wish we were back east so Inverno could have the opportunity for more book learning. She's a bright one too, Belva."

"Mama, I don't know why I never thought of it before, but it would be wonderful if Inverno could come back with me. She's just the right age for the Lockport Union School."

"Let's ask her," Mother said immediately.

Inverno was as excited as Mama. "Oh, Belva, I would love to be with you and to go on to school. I promise not to be any trouble."

"You'll be a big help to me with Lura."

This time the only objection Papa raised concerned Mama. "You're sure you won't be lonely without her?"

"Of course I'll be lonely, but that doesn't mean I can keep my children and grandchildren under my wing forever. If Belva thinks she can manage, I'll get Inverno packed right away."

It was a very happy threesome that boarded the train for New York State the next day. Lura was a grown-up seven-year-old who busied herself with her drawings on the trip back, but it was a help to have Inverno along when changing trains and settling luggage.

Belva made arrangements in Lockport to board in a pleasant home not far from the spacious campus overlooking the bustling town that had grown considerably in the thirteen years since she had thrilled to the trip on the Erie Canal. Lura's school was right across the street.

The water from the lockings had been diverted into a raceway that was the principal source of power for the city's growing industries. There were flour mills, textile mills, a barrel-stave plant, and a glassworks. The Rochester, Lockport, and Niagara Railroad connected with the canal route, and the town found itself the hub of commerce in western New York State.

Yet the harshness of progress was blunted by the beauty of the surrounding countryside. In the fall maples flamed in color, and fruit orchards puffed clouds of bloom on every hillside in the spring. The school itself was an example of modern construction. Belva was pleased to note that the city had not only provided fine gray stone buildings for the school, but they had also generously budgeted for splendid science laboratories.

One of Belva's first decisions was that all students be required to take an introductory course in science. Nineteenth century dreamers were making tremendous discoveries in all fields. Steam engines had already revolutionized transportation, and now the electromagnet had the potential to change industry. Not so very far away, Colonel Drake had drilled the first oil well in Titusville, Pennsylvania. Belva felt that boys and girls alike should be aware of the scope of these discoveries.

She planned frequent meetings with the staff of teachers to be sure that the level of instruction was of the highest quality. She insisted on their submitting an outline of their courses of study. The school was set up to provide a most inclusive three-year course for young people that would enable them to go on to college if they so desired, and of course she strongly urged this.

Belva also carried a full load of teaching herself, conducting classes in logic, rhetoric, botany, and higher mathematics. However, she rarely arranged to have Inverno enrolled in one of her classes. "The others would say I was playing favorites," she said.

Belva made a point of emphasizing class recitation as well as written assignments whenever possible. She explained at one of the faculty meetings, "I believe it is very important for young people to learn to express themselves verbally. Most of our communication is by word of mouth. I propose to teach a class in oratory for both girls and boys."

Many of the teachers objected to the radical idea that girls be included in the class. "It is unladylike. Debate makes for argument. Young women should still be seen and not heard," one of the older teachers said.

"I do not believe in sex distinction in literature, law, politics, or trade—or that modesty and virtue are more becoming to women than to men, but wish we had more of it everywhere."

Belva listened patiently to the criticism, but when she believed her ideas were right, she boldly went ahead to put them into practice. When she posted a notice on the bulletin board that a class would be offered to young ladies in public speaking, she found the classroom filled to capacity.

She explained, "We will start by memorizng a passage from literature, but later I will expect you to compose your own pieces for public speaking." Belva paced the floor, stressing that they should dramatize their orations with physical movement. "Make your words come alive. Captivate your audience with your own enthusiasm."

She closed the session with a thought that she made her own creed. "Words give us power. Use that power to make the world a better place in which to live." The class applauded.

During the first week of class Belva particularly noticed one young girl who mumbled her name in a flush of embarrassment when asked to stand and introduce herself. "Elizabeth Benner," she whispered and then edged back to her seat. Belva was surprised the young woman had had the courage to enroll in the course, but she was delighted. This was the sort of student who needed help the most.

By Thanksgiving Elizabeth had improved remarkably. She now held her head high, looked directly at her audience, and although her voice could never be heard in an auditorium, she was able to project her words in the classroom. Belva was so pleased that she penned a special note of praise on the report that was sent home to the parents of the students at Thanksgiving.

Almost immediately she was visited by Mr. Benner himself, a short man with a heavy black beard that exaggerated the proportions of his enormous head.

"Do I understand that you are making a spectacle of my daughter by permitting her to orate in front of an audience?"

"Don't you believe in women expressing themselves with words, sir?" Belva asked. "Would you have us be mute and communicate only by note?"

"It might be a most pleasant idea at times, madam."

Belva ignored his cutting remark. "Your daughter has gained poise and confidence with her brief training in speech class. Why, she might even choose a political career, sir."

She'd made the last statement in jest, but it had the desired effect to end the conversation abruptly. Mr. Benner turned on his heel and left the office. At once Belva was sorry that she had been so facetious. She expected that Elizabeth would not be permitted to return to class after that. It was true. Her chair remained empty, and no amount of persuasion could change Mr. Benner's mind, not even a personal note of apology from Belva.

One day as Belva was walking past the boys' athletic field, she paused to watch the young men go through their drill in calisthenics. With neat precision they waved their arms in windmill rotation. They bent in unison. They swayed as one.

"It is wonderful what rhythm they have developed," she said to their instructor, Mr. Freck.

The young man was pleased. "Not only does it improve their timing and coordination, but it helps to relax their muscles, stimulate circulation, increase appetite, and encourage proper health. Everyone should partake of such exercise, no matter what age."

"Or sex," Belva added. "Surely some of the simpler exercises could be performed by the girls. Others could be modified for our use. Mr. Freck, could you work out such a program?"

"Instruct young ladies in gymnastics?" His mouth dropped open.

"Why yes. I thought I understood you to say just now that everyone should follow such exercises."

"By everyone, I surely did not mean to infer the weaker sex, Mrs. McNall."

"I am not suggesting that we train the young ladies to build up their muscles but to relax them as you said," Belva continued.

"I emphatically do not agree with you, Mrs. McNall. It would be most inappropriate, and I am sure the plan would not receive the approval of the parents."

"The value of such exercise, of course, would have to be explained. I would need your help in formulating the ideas and the program of activity."

"I am sorry, madam, but I do not want to have anything to do with such nonsensical ideas."

"I will respect your wishes, Mr. Freck, but I do not mean to let you dissuade me from my idea."

Belva continued to watch the drill until the period ended, and in the privacy of her room that evening she and Inverno tried some of the exercises she had watched on the playing field. They did not seem too hard to perform and certainly exerted less strain than everyday household chores most women managed with ease. Lura watched her mother and aunt delightedly and joined in the fun. Together they worked out a routine of calisthenics that could be performed without any loss of modesty, without the need of any excessive strength.

Belva decided that she would conduct the class herself. Only those young women who expressed a desire to participate would be included, but on the first day, as it had been at the beginning of the public-speaking class, the students answered in large numbers. Belva was pleased to see how easily the young women caught on to the routines, how their grace and timing added to the pleasure of watching the drills. The boys stood around and laughed, but the odd sight of braids swirling from side to side and tiny waists bending nimbly to the count of "one and two, one and two" soon lost its novelty.

Such bizarre activities did not go unnoticed in the community. Mr. Benner was the first parent to withdraw his daughter from enrollment in the school. There were many protests, some verbal, some in writing, but Belva would not give up her idea to treat boys and girls as much alike as possible, giving equal advantages to both sexes. As the quality of education was so far superior to that of any other offered in the vicinity and as Belva had already earned many loyal friends, the school continued to operate at peak enrollment, patterned after Belva's own very individual ideas. The crisis had been met, and Belva had won.

Two years later she was asked to take over the head mistress's position at the Gainesville Female Seminary, which operated under the Mount Holyoke plan of combining study and housekeeping chores, thus defraying expenses and permitting almost any bright young woman to continue her education without the burden of financial debt. New challenges always interested Belva. She had reliable assistants in Lockport who could continue her philosophy of education there. She had new converts to make.

Inverno had earned her diploma and, with hopes of teaching in Illinois, had decided to return to her parents' home. So once again Belva and Lura packed their bags and moved on.

In 1859 the abolitionists were urging stronger and stronger penalties be imposed on the South. Few people from the northern states understood the Southerners' strength of conviction and fewer still understood the complex reasons for their differences. No one certainly expected a military confrontation. When the shot was fired at Fort Sumter, the news came as a shock to most citizens of western New York State. Still they felt that any army fighting such a just moral crusade against slavery would be able to win the war in a matter of days. As the weeks stretched into months and respected graduates of the United States Military Academy at West Point, Robert E. Lee among them, joined the side of the Confederacy, it became all too evident that the horrors of war would not be eased so soon.

As the young men, and soon older ones too, left for the fighting lines, women began to take over jobs that were strange to them. Farm women brought in crops and cared for livestock as well as children. The wife of the local cobbler cut out her first pair of shoes for her eldest son to wear when he left to join his father in the front lines. She was soon taking orders from others in the community, and it was said that she managed a better fit for customers than her husband ever did. The postmaster of Gainesville left his office in charge of his pretty young wife with the red braids. Mail was always sorted and bundled by noon. Without doubt, women were proving their ability, but when they attempted to compete in a man's world, they were frustrated, not only by local prejudice, but also by national laws prohibiting them from even putting their names to a legal document.

War brought about other changes. Meat was scarce, and there were few jars of preserves and vegetables on pantry shelves. What came fresh from the ground was hurried off to army soup kettles. No one traveled unless on emergency errands. The news that came by wire to the bigger cities and was transformed into newsprint for smaller communities was never current by the time Belva read it. Mama wrote that Warren had joined the regulars. Belva dreaded to read the lists of wounded and dead. A few months later she heard that her brother had returned home wasted by fever and dysentery. She said a prayer of thanks that at least his life had been saved.

Belva joined a group of ladies cutting, basting, and stitching uniforms for the volunteers. She continued to teach, but schools all over the country were forced to close or to cut down on classes as pupils were needed at home to take care of more important chores. Belva was fortunate that, as a college graduate and an experienced administrator, she was able to find employment, but she and Lura were forced to move two more times in the next two years, first to the Hornellsville Seminary and then to the Female Seminary in Owego, New York, on the banks of the Susquehanna.

Lura was now in her teens, a quiet young woman who shared her mother's love for books. Because of their many moves, she had made few close friends, but mother and daughter kept each other company. It was a close bond that was never to be broken during their lifetimes. They spent most of their evenings sitting opposite each other beside the oil lamp, reading. Lura owned several books of poetry that were her favorites. Belva poured over volumes of international law. She studied the Consular Manual. Only to Lura did she admit the preposterous thought that she might one day apply for some minor position in the foreign service of the State Department. She wished to travel when the war was over. Her eyes were still set on much broader horizons than Niagara County. Yet there was much to keep her involved at home, and she was never one to deny any help she could provide for others. One such incident set her sights in a different direction.

Belva was in the habit of arriving at her office to handle the detailed tasks of school administration before going to her classroom. The mother of one of her former students was waiting by her office one morning at an hour when the sun had barely slipped above the horizon. It was Mrs. Skott. Her daughter Clara had been an excellent student, but in the middle of the year she had dropped out of school without explanation. Belva had written to her urging her to continue her studies but had received no reply.

Clara's mother now stood before her dressed in mourning black. Belva felt guilty she obviously had not understood the family circumstances before. It was almost impossible to keep in touch with all her students, but it depressed her that her contacts were often impersonal, no matter how hard she tried to have it otherwise.

"I'm so sorry. I did not know of your loss," she said.

"Mr. Skott—he was with the 28th Regiment of New York Volunteers—was killed in action."

"You have my deepest sympathy, Mrs. Skott. I too have lost my husband and know what grief you are suffering. Please come into my office where we can talk."

Mrs. Skott seated herself in the straight chair opposite Belva's desk. "I am looking for a job, Mrs. McNall. I thought perhaps. . . ." She hesitated.

Belva shook her head sadly. "I wish I could help you, Mrs. Skott, but as you know our enrollment has dropped since the war started, and all our teaching positions are filled at present. I will surely keep you in mind if the situation changes."

Mrs. Skott nervously knotted the strings of the pouch purse she held in her lap. "I'm not qualified as a teacher, Mrs. McNall. I thought perhaps you might need cleaning help around the school. I don't know what else I can do. My husband owned the flour mill in town, but it was taken to clear our debts."

Belva looked up in surprise.

"I am in need of money," Mrs. Skott said simply.

"But surely you have received your widow's pension, haven't you?" Belva asked.

Mrs. Skott shook her head. "I have written to my husband's

commanding officer but haven't received a reply. I don't know where else to turn."

"I will certainly write a letter for you to the War Office in Washington. In the meantime, I will see if we can't find some suitable work."

"I thank you sincerely, Mrs. McNall. Clara was right. You are a wonderful woman."

"Don't thank me until we have found a permanent solution to your problems. This is not the first case that has come to my attention where military allotments have been delayed or canceled. We'll see about this even if it takes a letter to the President of the United States."

Belva kept her promise by sending four letters: to the War Office, to her Congressman, to the official listed as "Treasurer of the War Relief Fund," and, yes, to the President of the United States as commander in chief of the armed forces. Mrs. Skott promptly received the money due her.

Belva noted that each one of the letters had been addressed to Washington, D.C. Everything seemed to be handled in the nation's capital. If she just lived closer to Washington, she would be able to speak to Congressmen about the unfair practices she had often observed in the handling of women's affairs. Fairer laws must be passed. This thought continued to grow in the back of her mind, yet she hesitated. Travel was almost impossible because of the war.

Six months after her interview with Mrs. Skott, on April 2, 1865, Petersburg fell to the Northern Army led by General Grant. Shortly afterward General Robert E. Lee surrendered his forces, and peace, military peace, settled over an exhausted country. Now Belva could put her idea into action. She submitted her resignation as head of the Female Seminary in Owego. She packed her bags and bought train tickets to Washington, D.C., for herself and her daughter. She had no job in sight. Her savings would last only a few months, but Belva had made up her mind.

The nation's capital was to hear much of its new visitor.

Nine

It was a four-day trip, but Belva arrived refreshed, fired with enthusiasm for new conquests. The name Washington had a magic sound. She described her feelings to a friend. "I have arrived in Washington, this great political center, this seething pot where I can learn something of the practical workings of the machinery of government and see what the great men and women of the country feel and think."

It was not quite all that easy for a stranger to meet the great of Washington. She knew no one in the nation's capital, but she was not discouraged. This was where the decisions were made that ruled the people of the country and affected the people of the world. She aimed to have a part in framing this legislation. To make her voice heard, she was prepared to knock on doors, take to the podium, beat down the opposition by sheer determination. The opposition to what? She was as yet uncertain of all her aims, but she knew she would always fight for the right of women to be treated as equals with men.

She and Lura rented rooms in a boardinghouse conveniently located within walking distance of the Capitol. Frequently

Belva occupied a seat in the visitors' gallery of the Senate, taking note of the most influential politicians, men who gave some hint of support to legislation for equal rights.

Lura accompanied her mother at first but soon found other activities that interested her more. At seventeen Lura was an attractive young woman who was mature beyond her years. At first meeting she often gave the impression of being shy and reserved, but she was not unhappy. She was delighted that there was a free public library close by, and although Lura never shut herself away from the bustling activity of her mother's world, she cherished moments of solitude when she read her favorite poetry or filled notebooks with her own writing.

On the other hand, her mother rarely had a moment of solitude. Belva found to her delight that Washington, D.C., was the mecca for many dissenting groups with which she sympathized. It was a convention center that echoed the demands of dissatisfied minorities in the country. Belva scanned the newspapers for notices of public meetings. She immediately became involved in the women's suffrage movement. These stubborn women, who braved vicious criticism, also spread their banners for international peace. It would seem no hecklers could argue against this popular cause, but speakers frequently had to duck more than verbal brickbats. Aged eggs were favorite missiles. Belva was shocked at the indignities suffered by these zealous reformers.

At one such meeting she rose from her seat in the audience and made such a stirring speech denouncing the cruel physical attack on the speaker that the demonstrators left the meeting in shame.

Her ardent support and her ability to speak extemporaneously did not go unnoticed. Almost immediately she was asked to share the speakers' platform with other better known campaigners of the day. She never turned down such an opportunity, and often her day's schedule did not end until midnight.

Belva frequently voiced her criticism of some of these women campaigners, but only in the privacy of her own room and only to her daughter. "They bring ridicule upon themselves with their radical manners. And then no one will take their words seriously."

Belva was speaking of the unusual mode of dress adopted by some of the ladies, trousers topped by kilts or even pantaloons. Belva always remained her womanly self. Her clothes, while not of the most expensive silks and satins, were modishly cut and frivolously trimmed with fringe and bugle beads. She often wore flowers in her hair. Yet her speeches contained none of the more ornate phrases of oratory popular for the period. Her voice was said to be crisp and a bit nasal. She had trained herself to project her words to large audiences. Her speeches were always carefully outlined, organized with the clearest logic.

Belva met Julia Homes, a bloomer girl, who had just returned from climbing Pike's Peak, a first for women. Together they organized the Universal Franchise Association, with Belva as its first president. Already Belva was making her name known in the capital, and although she had not battered down the doors of the capital's leaders, she had introduced herself to several Congressmen. She presented them with letters framed in legal terms, suggesting specific legislation she felt the nation grossly needed.

Belva had traveled to Washington on a trial basis. Now that she had no doubts that her destiny lay here, she realized she must provide herself with an income that would allow her to stay and to make a more permanent home for Lura. Their transient life would have to end.

Belva inquired about a teaching position at Miss Hanover's Boarding and Day Academy. The salary offered was very meager and the hours she would have to work would mean a definite curtailment of her committee work and speaking engagements. It was Lura who came up with a possible solution one evening.

"Mother, why can't we start our own school? I could teach some of the subjects, and you would still have time to continue your other work."

"Why, Lura, that's an excellent idea. I believe we could do it if we planned our time together. I've met quite a few people in Washington who have children in need of college preparatory courses. I'll speak to Mabel Hochschild tomorrow. I would think that her daughter Agnes might want to enroll. I'm sure we can find suitable rooms to rent. I'll make inquiries tomorrow."

Belva immediately set about organizing their school for young ladies. She was able to rent space at the Union League Hall, a three-story narrow building on Ninth Street. Two rooms were set aside as classrooms, and across the hall she arranged living quarters for Lura and herself. The last of her savings was spent on desks and chairs and some very simple secondhand furnishings for their bedroom-sitting room. In the meantime, she posted notices that instruction would be given in science, philosophy, and other cultural subjects.

She was delighted that within a month she and Lura had all the students they could handle. Lura took over the teaching of French and Latin, and it was decided that they could afford to hire another young woman to spell Belva's teaching load when there was a conflict with her committee work. They also found it profitable to lease the schoolrooms in the evenings to religious, temperance, and political organizations. Everything seemed to be working out perfectly. Lura, too, was making friends, one in particular.

At the regular bimonthly meeting of the Universal Peace League, Lura was standing at the door of the assembly room passing out programs listing the speakers and the agenda for the meeting. A young gentleman formally introduced himself as DeForest Ormes and proceeded to ask a score of questions about the purpose of the organization, the length of time it had been in existence, and some of its accomplishments. When Lura was unable to provide all the answers before the program was to begin, the young man asked if he might stay for a few minutes following the meeting to gain more information. Lura agreed and seated herself at the rear of the room. Mr. Ormes conveniently discovered an empty chair next to hers.

While the two seemed to be listening attentively, both later admitted to each other laughingly that they could not possibly give even the most general summary of what was said that evening. Lura did remember, though, that when the meeting was over, Mr. Ormes changed his questions about the Universal Peace League to an invitation to the band concert the following Saturday. She hesitated but properly declined. Mr. Ormes, in turn, showed a proper air of disappointment and left. However, he returned the following evening to attend a temperance testimonial. In fact, Mr. Ormes suddenly developed an interest in all meetings held at the Union League Hall, and very shortly, whether there was a meeting or not, he was making his way to the building on Ninth Street. On Saturdays he and Lura usually walked in the park, stopping at the bakery shop after listening to the regularly scheduled outdoor concert. On rainy days they often made excuses to meet at the library. DeForest told her that, although he was a pharmacist by profession, what he really wanted to be was a scientist. He spoke of all the exciting things he felt were yet to be discovered through the use of electricity.

Lura told her mother proudly, "I'm sure that one of these days he will invent a really marvelous invention."

Belva laughed. "My darling, with your enthusiastic confidence, I am sure he'll be able to invent an invention."

But the courtship was not a hurried one, and it was Belva herself who went to the altar for the second time before her daughter. Belva met her husband-to-be not through any of her political activities but because of a toothache. She read an advertisement that Dr. Ezekiel Lockwood could "extract teeth without pain with nitrous oxide gas." He sounded like a young man with progressive ideas. She rang his bell and was surprised to discover that Dr. Lockwood's graying hair attested to more years of experience than she had guessed.

After introducing herself, she said, "I see that you practice modern scientific methods, Dr. Lockwood."

"You mean my use of anesthetics? Yes, I pride myself in reading the latest medical journals, and I occasionally attend classes to keep pace with the present and"—he smiled—"hopefully the future, but the world is changing so fast that I can promise you only yesterday's techniques."

"Can you really pull my tooth without pain?"

"What makes you think extraction is necessary?" he asked.

Belva hesitated. "I just thought that the only cure for an aching tooth was to get rid of that tooth."

"Mrs. McNall, I can see you have not kept up with dentistry journals yourself." He shook his head in jest. "So many patients want to prescribe their own treatment. Sit down please and let me examine your ailing tooth before I deliver sentence."

Belva smiled and followed the dentist's directions. After a brief examination she was relieved to hear that the tooth could be saved. With only a moment of mild discomfort, the tooth was treated and a filling prepared. A slight taste of oil of cloves was all that reminded her of the pain she had felt when entering the office.

"I'm most grateful, Dr. Lockwood." She paid her bill and turned to leave. Almost as an afterthought she turned to the kindly man with the sense of humor. "If you care to keep abreast of other issues, there will be a meeting this Friday at the Union League Hall which not only concerns women's rights but also equal rights for minority groups. I would be delighted if you could attend."

"That is certainly a challenging subject," the doctor replied. "I'll set aside the time, Mrs. McNall. Only the emergency of a patient's aching tooth will keep me away."

Belva was surprised at the excitement she felt while dressing for Friday's meeting. She spent particular time arranging her hair and at the last moment decided to add a spray of lily of the valley to the coil at the nape of her neck. People were already beginning to arrive. She could hear the shuffle of chairs in the meeting room across the hall. Perhaps she should save a seat up front for Dr. Lockwood, she thought. It would be unfortunate if he arrived late and was forced to stand in the aisle. They had announced an unusually fine program for the evening. Elizabeth Ashley would be the main speaker. Belva would preside.

When she entered the meeting room, she was surprised at the number of strangers who were already seated. Usually the faces were familiar to her, people who regularly attended the women's suffrage meetings. Tonight there was an unusual number of men present, men in rough clothing without the manners to remove their hats. As she scanned the audience, she was pleased to notice that Dr. Lockwood had already arrived. They exchanged smiles as Belva made her way to the front of the room.

Miss Ashley was already seated in one of the two chairs placed behind the low table that during the day served as the teacher's desk. There was really no reason to delay the opening of the meeting. The room was filled to capacity. As Belva rose to speak, someone in the back started to clap. He was joined by raucous hooting and the stomping of feet. The strangers Belva had noticed were deliberately causing the commotion. Her face reddened, first in a flush of embarrassment, then in anger. She waited a full moment for the room to quiet. The noise continued. Then she spoke as loudly as she could.

"Will you please be quiet so that we may hear what our good speaker has to say."

The noise continued at a louder pitch. She tried again. "Please, there are others here who have come to listen."

"I am one of them." Dr. Lockwood had risen from his seat. Turning to the troublemakers, he spoke with authority. "I plan to give the speaker my courteous attention and expect others to do the same. When she has finished, if there is disagreement, I'm sure time can be allotted for dissenting views."

He was applauded by many. A noisy demonstrator in the back shouted, "You go ahead and listen. If me and my friends want to make a bit of clatter, you aim you can stop us, you and your lady friends?"

Belva drew in her breath. Besides Dr. Lockwood, there were only three other gentlemen present, and they were so elderly that they could hardly have put up a physical fight to bring order. She would have to adjourn the meeting in defeat, but before she could put this action into words, Dr. Lockwood was again speaking.

"Perhaps you are not aware that we could easily sign a complaint for your arrest for disturbing the peace. If your intentions are to continue your present conduct, I will gladly take that measure."

A woman in the front row rose. "I know the names of two of the men who are causing this disturbance. They have tried to break up meetings before. I feel now is the time to take suitable action to prevent a repetition of their disgraceful behavior."

"If you will permit me, Mrs. McNall," Dr. Lockwood continued, "I will frame such a paper and ask every one of you to sign the complaint. Your names will bear weight with the office of justice."

The stamping and shouting stopped abruptly. Belva spoke. "If I may have your attention now, I believe we can continue without sending for the police. However, if there are any more interruptions, we will follow Dr. Lockwood's excellent advice."

As she was speaking, the hecklers got up one at a time and noisily left the room. The meeting proceeded as scheduled. Miss Ashley presented a lengthy list of reforms she felt necessary to adjust the legal inequities suffered by women. Then she turned her attention to the treatment accorded the Indian, who now fared worse than the black slaves who had been given their freedom, legally at least. No dissenting views were voiced, but several questions were raised from the floor. "Just what could citizens do to change conditions?"

Belva had a list of the names of Congressmen to write to. The meeting ended with a suggestion that these gentlemen should be invited to a meeting such as this one. Belva agreed, but she knew that few politicians wanted to become involved in issues of controversy. The most they could do was to popularize their cause by holding public meetings.

Belva joined Dr. Lockwood at the close of the meeting. "You came to our rescue at a most appropriate time. I sincerely thank you."

"I'm happy I could be of service. I had no idea you ladies had to put up with such uncivil conduct. There should be a way to keep these rowdies out, to reserve these meetings for the seriously concerned citizen."

"I wish I knew a way," said Belva. "We've thought of charging admission or issuing membership cards for attendance, but this defeats our purpose of attracting new converts."

"You may surely count on me as one of the converted, Mrs. McNall, although I don't believe that is the word to use. I've always believed that minority groups and women should be ruled, judged, and protected by the same laws as our white male citizens, but I have never given serious thought as to how this could be brought about."

"Our aim is to bring our cause to the attention of everyone in the country. Only then can pressure be brought to bear on our law-making representatives."

"You've opened my eyes tonight, Mrs. McNall. I hope you'll inform me of other meetings."

"I will surely do so, Dr. Lockwood, and again let me express our gratitude for your help this difficult evening."

Dr. Lockwood rarely missed a meeting of the reform committee. As he and Belva had a chance to see more and more of each other, their friendship deepened. Dr. Lockwood was considerably older than Belva, sixty-five years to her thirty-eight. He had been a widower for some time. Belva frequently relied on his strength, his encouragement, and his judgment to help her through crises.

He was a tall man, a kind man, possessing a sense of humor that reminded Belva of her father, but the doctor's education and travel had given him much more progressive ideas than Lewis Bennett. He had served as a chaplain during the war. Belva noticed several times that strangers turned to him for personal guidance, trusting his wisdom that could often sift contentment from the confusion of personal lives. He listened to others, was concerned for others. How different he was from Uriah, whose interests had always been more self-centered! But it was unfair to compare the two men. Each had admirable qualities. Perhaps the years had mellowed Ezekiel's traits.

Dr. Lockwood was much impressed with Belva's fine mind and her determination to fight for what she believed were her God-given rights. It was only natural that their mutual respect should turn to love.

On March 11, 1868, they were married. Dr. Lockwood gave up his offices in the Washington Building and set up his practice in the Union League Hall, down the corridor from the classrooms and his wife's office, which was almost always overflowing with campaigners for some reform issue.

Ten

Marriage did little to curtail any of Belva's activities. Lura moved into a boardinghouse nearby, but she remained very close to her mother and to her stepfather, whom she greatly admired. As Belva became more and more involved in reform committees, Lura took over the management of the growing school. She continued to see Mr. Ormes, but DeForest now had little time for courting. He was taking graduate courses in pharmacology and working long hours in a chemistry lab. Lura was busy with her own school routine. For the first time she was given full responsibilities. She loved it. She was an excellent teacher, and the girls adored her. Several stayed on even after they had completed the curriculum to form their own literary group.

Lura wrote poetry, which she frequently read to her mother. "I'm so proud of your sensitive, expressive use of words," said Belva. "You've inherited your father's fanciful imagination. I'm afraid my own nature tends toward science and fact. Never change, dear Lura. We both find happiness in people, but you are able to relax and enjoy friendships. I always seem to be driven to rush through life."

Lura smiled. "I may not be as relaxed as before, Mother. I'm going to write a column for the *Lockport Daily Journal*. I sent them a news item about your last meeting, and they've asked for a weekly bulletin on legislation sponsored by the Woman Suffrage Association, and even material on such frivolous matters as the social highlights of Washington for the women's page."

"That is wonderful, Lura. A lady reporter. You're pioneering in yet another field for women. And what an excellent opportunity you'll have to win support for our equal rights cause!"

Lura shook her head. "I'm not expected to editorialize, to write of my own feelings, just to report the facts."

Belva laughed. "Of course you're right. However, if a few words from one of our speakers are quoted in your column along with the color of her hat, it would help immensely."

They both laughed. "And may I quote you on that, Mrs. Lockwood?"

"I see I will have to be particularly careful of what I say."

Belva was very careful how she planned her words for the speakers' platform, but she confided to Ezekiel one time, "I feel I have said all that there is to say. I am repeating myself. No new words come to my mind. I should give up speaking."

"Those ideas are new to others, Belva. You told me yourself

that if you kept at the conscience of America, you were bound to succeed in winning the vote for women. Don't let our guilt feelings rest."

"You don't mind that I'm gone so often?"

"No, I'm proud to share your time because I share your hopes for a much more tolerant future."

Both Dr. and Mrs. Lockwood were disappointed that Congressman George Julian's proposal for "suffrage based only on citizenship" was defeated, but the very fact that the legislature was debating such an issue was a sign of progress. Belva continued an exhausting schedule of speaking engagements until it became evident that she was expecting a baby.

"Why, I'm old enough to be a grandmother," she said in dismay, "but how wonderful it is that Ezekiel and I can share in bringing up a family."

"I hope now you will promise to find time to relax," Lura said.

Belva smiled at her daughter's concern. "It will give me time to catch up on my correspondence."

Belva spent hours at her desk writing to people all over the country who were involved with the issue of women's rights. She asked questions: What support could be expected in state legislatures for a national referendum? Who were the leaders most tolerant of their views? Who could be counted on to chairman local committees? All the information she received was filed in a voluminous desk that seemed sure to overflow at any moment. Lura helped her mother answer some of the mail, but only as secretary taking dictation. Belva personally kept in touch with dozens of people all over the country.

In January of 1869 Belva gave birth to a baby girl. Dr. Lockwood at once announced that they would call the child Belva. "Such a beautiful child, Belva, and she'll undoubtedly inherit your mind."

"Are you sure you want another militant crusader in the family, Ezekiel?"

The doctor laughed. "I've been able to manage with one. I'm sure I'll get used to another."

"But, Ezekiel, I want her to be a gentle, dainty creature. I was thinking of calling her Jessie."

Dr. Lockwood nodded. "A compromise then. We will have a gentle crusader named Jessie Belva Lockwood."

Belva took her husband's hand and smiled. "I love you very much, Ezekiel."

Belva also loved her baby daughter very much and for the first two months would let no one share in her care. Yet as the requests for speaking engagements piled up on her desk, she became impatient to join the debate that was continuously taking place in one auditorium or another. More and more women were braving public criticism to organize for universal suffrage.

Lura came into her mother's office one morning to see Belva pacing the floor, delivering a lecture to an imaginary audience, with little Jessie snuggled contentedly in her arms.

Lura laughed. "Your audience is asleep, Mama."

Belva smiled. "I've just written a speech for Melissa Tandy to give. She is new to our party and said she'd feel more at ease with a prepared program for her first time in charge. I was practicing to hear how it sounded."

"It would sound fine coming from you, Mother. Why don't you deliver the address yourself?"

Belva looked at little Jessie resting against her shoulder. "And will you share the speakers' platform with me, little one?"

"I'd love to care for Jessie, Mother. You know it."

"It would be a great help to Melissa, and besides I have missed taking a part in the committee's work."

In a matter of weeks Belva was back on the lecture platform, still spending hours on correspondence and yet finding time to manage her household. Lura was a tremendous help, and the doctor was a devoted parent, enchanted by his tiny daughter, anxious to spend every moment he could spare in the nursery.

"Without you two wonderfully patient people I could never do it," Belva admitted.

"I've been thinking," Dr. Lockwood said, "that we should be looking for a more proper home in which to bring up our child. There are always a dozen people in and out of our rooms at all hours of the day. When Jessie is walking, there will be no way to keep her in control. And I am seriously thinking of retirement and would like quieter quarters for myself."

"You're right as always, Ezekiel. We'll start searching tomorrow."

"I've already looked at a house at 619 F Street. If it suits you, we could be moved within the month."

Within the week they had set up residence in the house that was to be Belva's home for many years.

In July of 1869 a newly formed organization called the Equal Rights Association of Washington had its first meeting in the third floor schoolroom of the Union League Hall. The primary purpose of the organization was "the securing of equal rights for all Americans regardless of race, color, or sex." Sixteen people representing whites and blacks, males and females, attended. None of the people there that day could have predicted what a long-range influence their words would have on the turn of political events.

Mr. John Crane, a prominent businessman, spoke. "For those who argue that women are the weaker sex, I would have them observe the physical capacities of black women who toil in the fields or frontier women who have made the trip across this continent in a covered wagon. If strength were the proof of the right to vote, there would be no question of their place in the polling lines."

"If we can again place this legislation before Congress," Belva said, "I believe that sentiment could be swayed in our favor."

"Do you think President Andrew Johnson would sign such a bill?" someone asked.

Mrs. Lockwood answered firmly, "I don't believe he would dare veto a suffrage bill if passed by Congress."

There were smiles. "That is still a pretty big *if*."

"Yes," Belva admitted, "but we cannot stop fighting until such legislation is passed, no matter what ridicule and humiliation we suffer doing so."

Those words were quoted in the next issue of the *Washington Star*.

"You've already won a round in your fight," Ezekiel said. "Such notice of your work, your words, stimulates the public's attention and surely generates support for your cause."

"And opposition," said Belva.

"You must take your own advice," Dr. Lockwood repeated. "Don't give up."

"You're right." Belva smiled. "We're planning meetings every week in our schoolroom."

Not all meetings were attended by sympathetic listeners, and Dr. Lockwood was not always there to help Belva keep order. At one such gathering two cabbages and a butter churn were rolled down the aisle. Belva was forced to adjourn the meeting in disgust.

"Class dismissed," she said. "If this were a schoolroom where you were the students, you would be expelled for your childish behavior."

Afterward at home, discussing the events with her husband,

she again confided her mood of depression. "I feel so foolishly incapable of handling the situation."

"My dear, no one could have done better. You cannot argue with those who will not listen."

"I feel that our only hope is to strengthen the power of the courts. The words of our Constitution have been forgotten by our elected officials, but what about our judges who are dedicated to uphold laws?" She hesitated. "Ezekiel, I have had some very serious thoughts I have been afraid to mention, for fear you would really think I had lost my mind."

"This is the first time you've failed to confide in me, Belva."

"I'm sorry, but I was sure you would laugh at me. I want to study law. I see no reason why a woman couldn't become a lawyer."

Dr. Lockwood hesitated only a moment while he thought of his wife's surprising words. "I think it is an excellent idea. You have the courage and the ability. What is holding you back?"

PART III

"My Cause Is the Cause of Thousands of Women"

Eleven

On October 23, 1869, Belva Lockwood applied for admission to Columbian College law school. Almost immediately she received a reply from President Samson. "We think the attendance of ladies would be an injurious diversion of the attention of the students."

Belva had expected opposition, but such a flimsy excuse annoyed her. Dr. Lockwood chuckled. "You should be flattered."

Belva refused to be amused. "I will send my application to every school in the country."

Georgetown University was the next to refuse her request with no reason given other than she was a woman and women had never been admitted. She composed a third letter addressed to Mr. William Wedgewood, Vice Chancellor of the new National University Law School in Washington. Mr. Wedgewood had often spoken openly in favor of women's rights. Belva intended to test his sincerity. She delivered her letter to him personally.

He was surprised but not dismayed at her request. "I don't believe that the university faculty will approve of the publicity that is bound to develop, but I'll speak in your behalf, Mrs. Lockwood."

It was several weeks before he gave her his disappointing answer. "As I surmised, the faculty has refused your admission as a student, Mrs. Lockwood, but I am willing to give you private instruction, and if other women are interested, I'll conduct classes in my office. However, you must understand this will not entitle you to a university diploma."

Belva was not dismayed. The first stumbling block had been overcome. She'd solve the other problems as they came. She started recruiting other young women for the study program.

Fifteen students enrolled in Mr. Wedgewood's classes. The professor admitted that they far excelled his male students in determination and concentration. Belva managed to keep up with her lessons by studying late into the night. Frequently she had only four or five hours of sleep, but she seemed to thrive on her exhausting schedule.

She could no longer count on Lura's help as she had in the past. Lura had set her own wedding date for the summer of 1869. Belva was delighted. She very much approved of her young son-in-law to be, DeForest Ormes, but it did mean she was busier than ever.

The wedding was attended by a large number of Washington friends, proof that Belva and Lura had found the capital city a hospitable place in which to settle and put down roots. Many people remarked that Belva and her daughter looked very much like sisters. A few gray strands threaded Belva's hair, but her energy far surpassed most women many years her junior. Extra demands on her time merely seemed to stimulate her, and even now there were new causes to support.

Remembering the unjust salary schedule for teachers in Royalton, she took on a new project, fighting for equal pay for female Civil Service employees. Men were often paid two or three times as much as women for an equal work load. Belva questioned many government agencies and came up with some discouraging statistics.

"Ezekiel, did you know that a woman cannot earn more than

seventy-five dollars a month as a Civil Service employee, and some of these women are trying to support families on this income?"

"That's a disgrace," Dr. Lockwood agreed. "Those facts ought to be brought to the attention of Congress."

"You're right, Ezekiel. Legislation is the only answer."

Belva immediately took her husband's advice. She drafted a bill that would equalize the salary structure of all Civil Service employees. After much persuasion, the Honorable J. M. Arnell of Tennessee agreed to present it to Congress, but he warned her, "Don't expect immediate results. The bill won't be out of committee for voting for several months."

In the meantime, Ezekiel and Belva decided to travel to New York City to attend the state and national conventions of the Woman Suffrage Association. Lura and her husband were willing to care for little Jessie, then only a year old. Belva made herself a new outfit for the trip and purchased a tiny blue saucer of a hat trimmed with feathers.

"You look charming, Belva, abolutely helplessly feminine." Ezekiel laughed. "I think it's unfair to deceive your opponents so blatantly."

"I see no reason why a woman should wear bloomers just to prove that she has intelligence. She's only adding to the myth that masculine habits are more desirable."

"You'll be the belle of New York," the doctor stated, and indeed she did make a striking figure.

She charmed many a prominent supporter of women's suffrage. She even enlisted the help of Horace Greeley, the well-known newspaperman.

"If you could occasionally concern your editorials with our women's crusade," she urged, "our message would be carried to hundreds more than we could ever hope to reach on the speakers' platform."

"You've convinced me, Mrs. Lockwood, that there's justice to be guaranteed here," he said. "You have my support."

Although she spent long days and evenings in meetings, she and Ezekiel found time to explore the exciting city. They rode on the horse cars that pushed their way through the crowded streets. Phaetons and hansom cabs jostled freight wagons. Sleek-looking horses and swayback nags nosed each other at every intersection. Theater marquees advertised the latest plays from England, and fashionable ladies of wealth, many dressed in furs, were seen shopping in the dozens of stores that crowded the lower tip of Manhattan. Belva bought herself a muff of soft beaver, and she insisted that the doctor purchase a handsome dove-gray weskit. She loved every minute of their visit, but she was not disappointed to leave. For her the real excitement was centered in the nation's capital, where the game of politics was being played.

As soon as she returned, she called on Mr. Arnell to learn when her Civil Service bill—and it could rightly be called hers—would be formally presented for vote. A date had been set. On March 21, 1870, she sat nervously in the balcony of the House of Representatives, listening to the words she had drafted read before the Congressmen. It was hard to restrain herself from springing to her feet to enter the debate. She heard the opposition claim that it was unfair to pay women an equal salary when men had to support families. She wanted to ask: What about widows and spinsters? Did a woman have to depend on the resources of a man for her substance? Shouldn't she have a choice and an equal opportunity to earn an equal living wage?

Belva held her breath when the roll was called and one by one the representatives spoke their yeas and nays. Belva kept her own count. It would be a close decision, but when the last vote was cast, she knew that the bill had passed the House of

Representatives. It must still be tested in the Senate, but Mr. Arnell assured her that opinion was favorable. His prediction proved true. The bill became law.

"Hereafter all clerks and employees in the Civil Service of the United States shall be paid irrespective of sex with reference to the character and amount of service performed by them." Belva had won her first legal battle in her lifelong fight for women's rights, the first piece of legislation ever to be passed by Congress to so designate those rights.

"I know it's not very modest of me, Ezekiel, to say that I'm proud of this accomplishment," Belva said, "but it's not conceit I feel, only pride that we've shown the public it is possible to correct injustice by legislation."

"You've set an important example," he replied.

"I know we can't abolish prejudice through laws, but we can set up guidelines for our actions by legislation. If women are given equal pay for Civil Service jobs, maybe other employers will do the same. There is so much to do." She turned to face her husband with a smile. "But I do intend to let others take much of the responsibility. I'm going to spend more time at home with my family. Ezekiel, you've been patient with me. Thank you."

"I hope you'll find time to rest, Belva. You've been setting yourself a killing schedule."

"I think Jessie will keep me just as busy. She is such an active little one. Lura never seemed to romp around so much." She laughed. "Or is it that I'm just getting older?"

Belva kept her promise and canceled almost all engagements that took her away from home. It was a good time, a happy time. Ezekiel often read aloud in the evening as Belva stitched a new dress or petticoat for Jessie, who was growing so fast that her baby clothes no longer fit her. "Running and growing, that's what she does best," said Belva. "I'm glad."

It was strange then to see her quiet one day. Belva found her curled up in a living room chair. The little girl had not moved for almost an hour.

"Are you feeling all right, darling?" Jessie didn't answer. "You must be tired, little one. You played so hard this morning."

Gently Belva lifted Jessie into her bed and let her sleep. Little Jessie awoke several hours later with a raging fever. Her eyes gazed without focus. Belva applied cold compresses to the child's body and walked the floor with her until Ezekiel returned during the gray dawn with a doctor.

Dr. Logan bent over the child and examined her. It was not long before he turned to the parents, his face grave. "It is typhoid fever."

"Oh no." Belva's breath caught in her throat. "What can we do to help her, doctor?"

He shook his head. "There's little anyone can do, Mrs. Lockwood. You were right to swathe her in damp cloths to fight the fever. I'll be back tomorrow."

Belva would not permit anyone to take over Jessie's care during the nightmare of fever that lasted three days and three nights. Lura brought food to her mother's room, but Belva had no appetite. Ezekiel tried to console her, but it was no use. When death came to the little girl, Belva was so drained of energy that she sat in numb silence, unable to relieve her grief with tears. Was there anything she might have done to ward off the illness? The doctor assured her nothing could have prevented the tragedy.

For more than a week Belva kept to her room, staring at nothing, trying to think of nothing, to help erase the grief that tightened a band of pain at her temples and the base of her neck. Yet she knew that she must force herself to continue her life, her work. Again she turned to her law books and went back to her classes and to her meetings. She filled every minute of her time trying to forget her personal tragedy.

While in New York, Belva had met Victoria Woodhull, a young woman who, with her sister, had opened a brokerage office on Broad Street. The press had published many amusing comments regarding the lady bankers and some harsh criticism of their personal conduct, but Belva had been impressed with the sincerity and competence of Mrs. Woodhull. The lady from New York was urging women to test their right as citizens, guaranteed under the Fourteenth Amendment, by registering to vote and bringing suit in the courts if they were refused.

On the day of registration Belva and Lura met with seventy other suffragettes to march through the streets of Washington to the office of the registrar. They were immediately ordered to disperse.

"We are American citizens," Belva protested, "and, as such, have been guaranteed the right to vote by the Constitution of the United States of America."

The official in charge again denied them this right. "I take my orders from the Election Commissioner."

"And where is he?" Belva demanded.

"Out of the city, ma'am."

It was obvious that no action could be taken that day. Only the courts could decide the justice of the case, but it was Susan B. Anthony, not Mrs. Lockwood, who finally stood trial during the test case. Miss Anthony had managed to vote in the November 1872 election in New York State.

In Miss Anthony's own words written to her friend Elizabeth Stanton she said: "Well, I have gone and done it . . . positively voted the Republican ticket, straight this A.M. at 7 o'clock." Two weeks later she was arrested by a United States deputy marshal. The case came to trial on December 23 in

Rochester, New York. She was found guilty and fined a hundred dollars. Miss Anthony replied that she would not pay one cent to the government. Her lawyer paid the fine without her knowledge, and she was released. She was furious that, with the fine paid, she was denied the right to appeal the case before the Supreme Court.

However, the publicity had brought much sympathy to the cause, and Belva was delighted that Susan had stood her ground in court. "Because of her, the battle will not be so long," Belva said to her husband.

Belva was ready to start a battle of her own. By May 1873 she had finished her course of study at the National University Law School. Mr. Wedgewood delivered the news he had predicted. "I cannot offer you a diploma, Mrs. Lockwood."

"Does this mean that I failed the examination?" Belva asked.

"No, on the contrary, I would say that you were one of the most outstanding students it has been my privilege to supervise. I am sure you can guess the reason. The majority of the faculty do not approve your desire to follow a career in law. It is unfair, Mrs. Lockwood, but there is nothing I can do."

These words again acted as a challenge. "I will not give up," she said firmly, and anyone seeing her mouth set with determination and her shoulders squared for battle could well have predicted the outcome. Her next adversary was none other than the President of the United States, Ulysses S. Grant, who by virtue of his office, was also the titular head of the National University Law School. He rarely took a hand in any of the school's affairs, and surely he must have been more than a little surprised when he received a personal letter on September 3, 1873.

"You are, or you are not, the President of the National University Law School. If you are its President, I wish to say to you that I have passed through the curriculum of study of that school, and am entitled to, and demand my Diploma. If you are not its President, then I ask you to take your name from its papers, and not hold out to the world to be what you are not."

Mrs. Lockwood received no reply to her letter, but within a week she was granted the Degree of L.L.B. signed by the faculty and by President Grant. There was no ceremony, no cap and gown graduation. The diploma was delivered by a postman, but she read and reread it.

"I'm so very proud for you," Ezekiel said. Then he added with a twinkle in his eye, "Do you know this makes me the very first husband of a lawyer, the very first?"

At forty-three years of age Belva Lockwood was about to start on a new career as the first woman lawyer in the history of the United States.

On September 24, 1873, she was admitted to the Bar of the Supreme Court of the District of Columbia, and shortly after she was arguing cases before this astute body. Her first client was Mrs. Mary Ann Folker, whose "prayer" for divorce was entered before the court, charging Mr. Folker with drunkenness, cruel treatment, and desertion.

"There has been no testimony to contradict that this poor woman has been treated worse than a slave. Yet her master does not even provide her with food and shelter. You call women the weaker sex, but you do not give them protection in this world where they are barred from earning a living. Do you not feel shame that men have brought women to such a sorry state of degredation?"

Belva won the case, obtaining the divorce for her client and a court judgment that the ex-husband pay for the woman's support until she could find gainful employment. The judge, however, told her that there was no law to make the defendant pay. Belva refused to believe him. She took the case to court again, this time as a simple collection of debt. The jury was once more impressed with Belva's words, and the man was clapped in prison until he did pay.

Belva opened an office in her home. It was the year 1873, a time of financial panic and political scandal. The poverty of industrial workers in the big cities was appalling, and the number was swelled each day with immigrants from abroad. The cost of the Civil War and the government's financial support in building railroads had almost bankrupted the national treasury.

It was not the best time to be starting a new law practice, Belva was warned, but from the first, she found that she was swamped with work. Lura turned her duties at the school over to a friend and became Belva's part-time secretary, although she had proudly announced that she was soon to have a baby. Dr. Lockwood gave up his dental practice to become a notary public and claim agent. Although the family was busier than ever, they had more time to be together, sharing problems, victories, and defeats, and when little Inez was born, her cradle often was trundled into her grandmother's busy office.

Belva's work included all kinds of property and account cases, settlements, injunctions, and especially claims against the United States government. One of the earliest cases that brought her publicity and notoriety was her defense of an accused murderess.

Belva's client described on the witness stand how she had happened to commit the crime of shooting a constable. Mrs. Lockwood's defense was superb. She rose before the court and said, "Gentlemen of the jury, the laws must be enforced. My client has committed the double offense of resisting an officer of the law and shooting a man. The District is under the common law. That law says a woman must obey her husband. Her husband told her to load a gun and shoot the officer. . . . I claim you are not trying the right prisoner. You would not have a woman resist her husband?"

The jury reached a verdict of "not guilty" in record time. Belva hoped that this ridiculous argument for the defense would lead people to consider the double standard they imposed in their laws, but most of the talk revolved around Belva's "smart aleck" behavior, snickered at by some, disapproved of by many, supported only by a slim minority.

Belva had no intention of serving only women in her law practice, but there was no doubt, however, that few men approached Belva for her services. They were bound to be open to ridicule. This did not mean that Belva was idle. To the contrary, for the first time women had a sympathetic champion who took on cases whether payment was guaranteed or not.

One of the clients she represented was the widow Charlotte VonCort, who was suing the United States government for the infringement of a patent for a torpedo boat invented by her late husband. The case was won in a lower court but appealed before the United States Court of Claims. Belva was not allowed to plead her case in this court without special permission. She at once asked to be admitted but was refused. She then took her own case to court stating that she had been unfairly discriminated against.

Justice Nott stated the court's case simply. "Mistress Lockwood, you are a woman."

Belva at once pleaded guilty to the charge, and the Chief Justice announced that the case would be continued for one week while he had time to ponder the weighty problem. On the following week she again marched into the courtroom. This time the words of the judge were even more explicit.

"Mistress Lockwood, you are a married woman. A married attorney might possibly misapply funds of a client. Under our common law of today, a husband could rightly be held responsible for the wrong his wife had committed as a lawyer. I cannot take such a risk by approving your presence in this courtroom in the capacity of attorney."

Instead of giving up, Belva decided to take her plea a step farther by applying for admission to the Supreme Court of the United States, the highest court in the land. It would be an unexpected tactic. Surprise might be in her favor. Opponents to this appointment had not had a chance to build strong barriers. She sat down to make a list of people to whom she would write for support. Ezekiel would have some suggestions. She hurried to his office.

When she opened the door, she saw that he was slumped with his head on his desk. He had been working too hard himself, she thought. He should be enjoying retirement at his age. She started to leave, letting him have his rest. Then suddenly she stiffened with fear. Was he ill? She rushed to his side and found he had lost consciousness. His breathing was shallow, his color ashen. She screamed for Lura, then rushed out the door to summon a doctor.

When she returned, his eyes were open, but it was evident that he had suffered a stroke. During Belva's lifetime it always seemed that tragedy struck when least expected. The doctor assured her that with intensive care Ezekiel would recover. She said a prayer of thanks. Again she canceled all of her business appointments. She made up a pallet for herself next to his bed and prepared all of his meals when he could take nourishment.

Slowly he regained his strength, although his right leg was affected with some paralysis. He spent most of his time in a bed or in a chair by the window. During the day she sat beside him either reading to herself or, when he felt like visiting, chatting about letters she had received from people all over the country who frequently asked her legal opinion on how best to fight the local laws of prejudice.

"You are needed in court much more desperately than in the kitchen," Ezekiel remarked. "Surely we can hire a housekeeper to take care of my wants."

Belva shook her head. "I'm enjoying myself, Ezekiel, selfishly satisfying my own self."

"I thank you for putting it that way," he answered, "but I insist. Soon you will be restless, and it is foolish to waste our combined energies in an invalid's room."

Belva reluctantly took his advice. Baking biscuits was not her best talent. Martha Applebe joined the household and relieved Belva of some of her responsibilities. Still she took on only the more important cases presented to her. She could handle her correspondence at home. Much of it was directed to her goal to be granted permission to argue cases before the United States Supreme Court.

Dr. Lockwood made a wise suggestion. "I believe you'll have a better chance of success by submitting your case to Congress. Only through legislation will the court acknowledge your rights."

Belva reached for her husband's hand. "Ezekiel, you do a great deal to bolster my strength when it is sagging."

"My dear, if it sagged a trifle less, I cringe at the thought of the state of our nation." They both laughed. The day was a happy one.

At once she began to marshal her campaign. "I'm sure Mr. Wedgewood will talk to some of his friends in Congress for me, and I will call Mr. Riddle myself."

The exact wording of the petition was most important. Belva spent hours composing, changing, discarding phrases that would state her request—no, her demand.

"To the Honorable the Senate and the House of Representatives in Congress assembled, Mrs. Belva A. Lockwood, attorney at law of Washington, D.C. . . . . adult licensed to practice before the bar of the Supreme Court of the District of Columbia, prays that these Honorable Bodies speedily pass a Declaratory Act to the effect that no woman otherwise qualified shall be debarred from practice before any United States court on account of sex." With the petition, she presented a brief referring to such precedents as Queen Victoria and asserting the "right to practice law" was one of the privileges of citizenship. On May 25, 1874, the petition was referred to the Senate Committee on the Judiciary. The unwinding of red tape was just beginning. At times the snarls seemed impossible to unravel.

Ezekiel continued to improve, and within a month Belva was working as hard as ever on her legal practice and committee work. One of her closest friends was Mary Walker, a practicing physician, who had provided heroic service during the Civil War, ministering to the wounded from both North and South. Dr. Walker always wore black pantaloons and frock coat, a cane hooked jauntily over her arm. Belva disapproved of such affectation, but she admired the lady doctor immensely. On occasion Dr. Walker dropped by to see Ezekiel, but as he rarely needed her professional services, she and Belva would gather in Dr. Lockwood's room, their conversation surely turning to political matters.

Belva also consulted frequently with Lucretia Mott, who had now reached an age when she should have been sitting peacefully in her parlor knitting and listening to grandchildren, and Elizabeth Cady Stanton, who had organized the first Woman's Rights Convention in 1848. Now they were planning their convention for the memorable year 1876.

Twelve

To mark the one hundredth anniversary of the founding of the United States, a World's Fair was to be held at the birthplace of its founding, Philadelphia. Politicians and businessmen were busy arguing over what displays would best represent the new nation's progress during its first one hundred years. Funds were collected to put up impressive buildings and assemble exhibits. Pride of accomplishment was strong, but Belva Lockwood and a group of suffragettes were not satisfied. They pointed out that one hundred years after the signing of the Declaration of Independence, women were still deprived of their basic rights of citizenship. Their freedom was still to be won.

It was more than a slight embarrassment to the government that they should be so vocal with their complaints at a time when politicians were trying to present a glowing image of the country. Knowing that this was an excellent time to gain a hearing for their cause, the young women, and many not so young, formed a committee to draft a Declaration of Women's Rights, which they hoped to read on July 4, 1876, at the height of the centennial celebration.

Matilda Gage, who had been editing a detailed account of the *History of Woman Suffrage*, was selected as chairman, but

Belva was asked to phrase the ideas as a legal document. She had spent every evening for a month at her desk. Now her work was finished and the delegation from Washington was ready to leave, but she hesitated. Ezekiel was not well. She worried about leaving him during the heat of summer. Dr. Lockwood made the decision.

"The attention of the public will focus on Philadelphia this July 4. You would be foolish to miss this opportunity for such an audience." He smiled. "My dear Belva, unless you are more a miracle woman than I have guessed, you will not be able to attend the bicentennial in 1976, so snatch this opportunity while you can."

"Are you sure you'll be all right, Ezekiel?"

"Of course. I hate to disappoint you, but Martha bakes just as good biscuits as you do."

Belva laughed. "'Better I'm sure. Then I'll pack my bags and write to Miss Anthony that I am on my way."

Susan Anthony had already set up headquarters for the National Woman Suffrage Association in the parlors of a home at 1431 Chestnut Street. A steady stream of visitors found her doorstep. She was delighted to see Belva, but she greeted her with disappointing news.

"They've told us we cannot present our declaration during the official program. In fact, it has been impossible to secure tickets for seats within hearing distance of the speakers' platform." Her austere manner broke for a moment as she smiled slyly. "Only through devious means was I able to obtain one ticket, which I hope to use for myself. I managed to get a press card as a reporter for my brother's paper the *Leavenworth Times*, under the name S. Anthony. I'm sure they have no idea who that reporter is, but I'm willing to use every advantage for our worthy purpose."

"As a reporter, you will be seated directly on the speakers' platform. Is there any chance you might arise and deliver our memorandum before there are objections?" Belva asked.

Susan Anthony hesitated thoughtfully. "Surprise would be to our advantage."

"I intend to station myself some place in Independence Square where I can see you, Susan, even if your words, which I know by heart, are lost to me."

Belva knew that if anyone could manage to deliver their message it would be Susan B. Anthony. She left her suitcase and hatbox at the suffrage headquarters and went out to see the fair.

The main exhibit hall was impressive, almost two thousand feet long and nearly five hundred feet wide. She wandered through Machinery Hall with its hydraulic fountain and industrial exhibits from all over the world. She was also interested in the foreign cultural buildings. A Chinese pagoda was placed next to a mock Venetian canal. It was almost as if she were traveling around the globe. Sometime she would cross the ocean, she told herself, sometime.

She had come to see the Women's Pavilion designed by twenty-two-year-old Sophia Hayden. The building was most adequate, Belva thought, and charmingly designed. It was painted a light blue, its center dome decorated in an ornate pattern of pastel colors. But inside came the disappointment. She found only displays of women's contributions to the arts: needlework from Italy and France, wood carvings from Germany. There were flowers made of fish scales and pictures made of human hair and a portrait bust of Queen Victoria carved out of butter. What of the more important contributions women had made, building the country, developing industry? Surely an exhibit could have been planned to display the skilled work of women in the prosperous shoe and textile industries. And they worked in the manufacture of dozens of products, from cartridges to Waltham watches. Wouldn't it have been appropriate to have a gallery of honor for the professional women who had succeeded in proving that women could take over many occupations thought to be the sole province of men? It was further proof that they needed to voice their demands loud and clear. Tomorrow would be the day. The multitudes would assemble and they would hear from the weaker sex.

The sun beat down unmercifully from a cloudless sky. Shafts of heat reflected from rooftops and glinted fire from the gun muzzles slanted precisely over the shoulders of soldiers standing smartly at attention. By early morning crowds had already begun to jostle for position before the huge speakers' stand set in front of Independence Hall. Bunting draped the impressive building, and flags hung limply from tall poles that spiked the four corners of the square.

Belva stood with a friend, Marilla Ricker of New Hampshire, to the right of the reserved seats, but still within hearing distance of the rostrum. Mrs. Stanton and Lucretia Mott had refused to attend the celebration so indignant were they over the snubs women had received from the Centennial Committee. They had chosen instead to hold their own meeting at the First Unitarian Church.

"They'll only attract an audience already sympathetic to our cause. We should aim for a new audience," Belva had said, and she was here to see if Susan Anthony would be able to make good her promise that with or without permission she would read the Declaration of Women's Rights.

Belva's companion was a young widow and law student who had registered and voted in the New Hampshire election of 1870. Mrs. Ricker claimed this right as a property owner, but her vote was refused. She and Belva had corresponded regarding the legal testing of the case. Now they stood shoulder to shoulder in the heat, waiting with anticipation for the program to start.

At exactly ten o'clock the privileged few who were to share the speakers' platform marched up the steps and took their seats.

Belva touched Mrs. Ricker's arm in surprise. "Why, Marilla, am I seeing right? Aren't there five women in that group? I thought Susan Anthony was the only one to obtain a ticket."

"Maybe the committee has had a change of heart."

Belva, on tiptoe, strained to get a better look at the five feminine hats that contrasted abruptly with the gentlemen's towering silk hats. "There's Susan all right and Matilda Gage, Lillie Black, Sarah Spencer, and, yes, Pheobe Couzins. She has certainly chosen the most militant of our group to share her honor. I wonder if that is wise."

General Hawley, master of ceremonies, arose and signaled the musicians to play the new overture that had been composed especially for the occasion. Then there was the introduction of Thomas W. Ferry of Michigan, acting Vice President, who had been chosen to represent President Grant. The benediction was delivered by the Reverend William Bacon Stevens. Belva held her breath. Susan Anthony would have to make her move soon.

The next speaker on the program was Richard Lee of Virginia, grandson of one of the signers of the Declaration of Independence. It was an impressive moment when the time-honored document was held aloft for the cheering crowd to see.

Slowly and solemnly he read the familiar words: "When in the course of human events . . ." When he closed, "We mutually pledge to each other our Lives, our Fortunes and our sacred Honor," the crowd erupted with cheers and applause that lasted for a full five minutes. During the enthusiastic confusion Susan Anthony made her way past the other dignitaries on the speakers' platform until she reached the side of Vice President Ferry.

"She's done it," said Belva triumphantly.

"But will they let her read it?" said Marilla.

Susan Anthony was not to be denied. The crowd began to quiet as they became aware of the drama taking place in front of them. Susan's voice could now be heard as she said, "I present to you a Declaration of Rights from the women citizens of the United States." She handed the surprised gentleman the document and proceeded to read from her own copy. The crowd strained to hear her words.

She ended with, "We ask equality. We ask justice. We ask that all civil and political rights that belong to citizens of the United States be guaranteed us and our daughters forever."

Belva's own clapping was drowned by the cheers around her. Not everyone perhaps was shouting for the sentiments voiced but rather for the courage of the indomitable woman standing before them in her Quaker gray.

"She was splendid, magnificent," said Belva. She felt a selfish twinge that she had not been a part of the dramatic presentation, but she had played much the same role as Thomas Jefferson had one hundred years ago, framing thoughts in ringing words. "Wait until Ezekiel and Lura hear about this."

The ladies had not yet finished their day of celebration. Those on the platform led a procession, at the same time distributing printed copies of the Declaration of Women's Rights throughout the crowd, to the First Unitarian Church, where the women's suffrage meeting was in progress. The church was already filled, but room was made for the newcomers and the program continued.

Mrs. Lucretia Mott, a fragile little woman in her eighties,

slowly climbed the winding staircase to the octagonal pulpit. "I climb this pulpit," Mrs. Mott began, "not because I am of lofty mind but because I am short of stature."

Laughter eased the tension, but the words that followed were solemn. One by one the members of the committee rose to comment on the various points mentioned in the document. Belva Lockwood was called upon to say a few words. She spoke of the role of the judiciary system of the United States.

"It has proved itself only the echo of the party in power. Women must be given the right to vote so that we may elect fine upstanding representatives to govern the country. Our judges cannot be allowed to play party politics. As it stands now, their interpretation of laws unsettles our faith in their authority."

The meeting lasted for five hours. The famous Singing Hutchinsons closed with the popular ballad:

> *"One hundred years hence what a change will be made,*
> *In politics, morals, religion and trade.*
> *In statesmen who wrangle or ride on the fence*
> *These things will be altered a hundred years hence.*
>
> *Then woman, man's partner, man's equal will stand*
> *While beauty and harmony govern the land.*
> *To think for oneself will be no offence,*
> *The world will be thinking a hundred years hence!"*

Thirteen

Although Belva might have fretted that she had missed the speakers' platform for the dramatic centennial celebration, she missed very few other opportunities to make herself heard. Her name had become familiar to hundreds of people. Her words were quoted, her actions reported. Most assuredly Belva enjoyed being on center stage, but there is no doubt that her primary purpose for public debate was her sincere conviction that women must fight for their legal rights.

She was the principal speaker the following year at the national convention of the Woman Suffrage Association. "I have been told," she said, "that there is no precedent for admitting a woman to practice in the Supreme Court of the United States. The glory of each generation is to make its own precedents. As there was none for Eve in the Garden of Eden, so there need be none for her daughters on entering the colleges, the church, or the courts."

In her velvet dress and train, her eyes blazing with indignation, she marched up and down the platform. As was reported in the paper, "She might have fairly represented the Italian Portia at the bar of Venice. No more effective speech was ever made on that platform."

Belva returned home excited and anxious to talk over the events of the week with her husband. He listened attentively, nodded frequently in agreement, but he seemed utterly exhausted, not able to carry on a discussion. Belva suggested they retire early. On the twenty-third of April Dr. Lockwood died in his sleep.

Belva had slipped out of bed early as was her custom and had finished her own breakfast before preparing a tray for Ezekiel. When she entered their room again, she opened the curtains and turned to speak to her husband. When he didn't answer, she rushed to his side. She touched his hand. Already it had lost the warmth of life. She felt his pulse. Now she knew the truth. She need not call the doctor. The end had come peacefully, but it might as well be the end for her, she thought.

Belva knelt beside his bed and pressed his hand against her dry eyes. For almost an hour she sat in their room trying to compose her thoughts, her own trembling hands. Few would have guessed the helpless terror she, Belva Lockwood, felt, she who had always appeared so self-sufficient. Few realized the deep attachment she and Ezekiel had shared. While not seen in public frequently, Dr. Lockwood had been a well of encouragement to which Belva came when her own resources ran dry. His suggestions had often set her course in the right direction.

Belva now felt more alone than ever before in her whole life. Lura was her only family now. She had lost contact with Royalton. Warren wrote occasionally, and she had heard of her mother's death only after the burial. She had many acquaintances but so few in whom to confide.

It was Lura and DeForest who took care of the funeral arrangements. Belva sat at her desk, but her mind wandered and her pen remained in its stand. She accepted no callers. She would talk only to Lura.

"Why don't you come to live with us, Mother? DeForest and I have plenty of room."

"Not with the news you told me last month that I'm going to

be a grandmother again," said Belva. "I'm delighted for you, but at this time in my life I must be alone with my thoughts."

"Please don't say it that way, Mama. So many people depend on you. Ezekiel would not have wanted you to despair. One of the most important bits of advice he gave to you was that you should fight for your Supreme Court appointment by proposing legislation in Congress. It has been weeks since you wrote to any of the Senators about their sponsoring such a bill. You've never given up on a fight before."

Belva looked up surprised. "No, I haven't and neither did Ezekiel. You're right, Lura. I'll answer Senator Sargent's letter today. He was the last to give me hope that he would present such a bill, although he would not assure me of his help."

"Whatever happened to the petition you were circulating among the lawyers of Washington?" Lura continued.

"It is here someplace in my desk, and it contains an impressive list of signatures from some of the finest men in the country."

Again Belva lost herself in work to try to blunt the edge of grief. She carefully drafted a bill stating that "any woman who shall have been a member of the bar of the highest court of any State or Territory or of the Supreme Court of the District of Columbia for the space of three years, and shall have maintained a good moral character, shall, on motion and the production of such record, be admitted to practice before the Supreme Court of the United States."

She sent the document and the petition signed by 155 lawyers of the District of Columbia to Senator Aaron Sargent. The senator was duly impressed. As a powerful machine politician from California, he had sufficient influence to place her bill, now labeled H.R. Number 1077, on the Congressional calendar for vote. However, it was not until February 1879 that the bill was brought to debate on the floor of the United States Senate.

Belva Lockwood sat nervously in the Senate gallery. Her face was drained of all color. She felt a weakness in her knees, but there was nothing further she could do to win her battle. It was in the hands of the fifty-nine men seated below her.

Senator Sargent's words were moving. "Women have the same right to life, liberty, and the pursuit of happiness and employment, commensurate with their capabilities, as a man has. As to the question of capacity, the history of the world shows from Queen Elizabeth . . . to Mrs. Stowe that capacity is not a question of sex."

Now Senator George F. Hoar of Massachusetts rose to speak. Belva knew that he was an advocate of women's rights, but what new issue could he raise to sway the minds of his colleagues?

He smiled affably. "Gentlemen, this is not a bill merely to admit women to the privilege of engaging in a particular profession. It is a bill to secure for the citizen of the United States the right to select his own counsel. You would not have your own rights to make this selection be limited, gentlemen, I am sure."

On February 7, 1879, more than five years since she had started her case, the bill was passed by the Senate with thirty-nine yeas, twenty nays, and seventeen abstaining. The bill had passed the House the year before, and on February 15 it was signed by the President. The five years of hard work to gain that victory were forgotten. Belva sent bouquets of flowers to the senators who had championed her cause.

The editor of the New York *Nation* commented on the floral gifts. "This is a pleasing omen of that purification of legal business which it is hoped will flow from the introduction of women to the courts. . . . It is pleasant to think of the oratory of 'favorite sons' being stimulated by the gentle rivalry as to which of them shall get the most bouquets or the biggest basket of flowers, instead of those lower motives which have had such full play heretofore."

At one o'clock on March 3, 1879, Belva stood between her two sponsors, Judge Samuel Shellabager and the Honorable Jeremiah Wilson, before the august body of judges of the United States Supreme Court. A newspaper reporter in the gallery scribbled in his notes that Mrs. Belva Lockwood looked frail and nervous. Anyone knowing the indomitable lady would have allowed that she might at this moment be feeling a twinge of nervous excitement, but never would they have described her as frail.

She stood solemnly listening to the order being read that admitted her to the bar of the highest court of the land. Yes, she did feel nervous. So much depended on her own conduct. In the public eye she was a representative of all her sex. If she should falter, those who sought these same privileges of equality would have to fight twice as hard for them. She must remain an example of womanly grace and prove intelligence and capability heretofore attributed only to men. She must combine softness and strength, modesty and aggressiveness, a contradiction not expected of any male lawyer.

The nine judges sat on a raised platform before a gleaming slab of mahogany that served as a common desk for all. The platform itself was fenced by an ornate balustrade. Behind the judges, marble columns marched in an impressive line the width of the high vaulted room. Directly behind the chair of Chief Justice Morrison I. Waite, an arched opening was hung with wine-red velvet. Above the arch a golden eagle hovered on a pedestal, as if about to soar in attack against any who might question the decisions of the presiding sages.

Chief Justice Waite rose and made his way to the end of the dais. The court clerk came forward from his station half hidden by an enormous roll-top desk at the left. He held in his hand a heavy, handsomely tooled leather-bound Bible. Belva placed her small gloved hand on the sacred volume and repeated the oath that she would uphold the justice of the court to the best of her ability. Her voice was strong. She clipped her phrases precisely.

When the last word was spoken, Chief Justice Waite and her sponsors warmly offered their congratulations. Many others crowded around to shake her hand. Belva blushed with pride, but she knew many approached her out of curiosity rather than because they approved. She was now a mature woman of forty-eight, twice a widow, a grandmother of two. Another baby girl, this one named Rhoda, had joined the Ormes family. But Belva was about to assume new responsibilities in her life. She wished with all her heart that Ezekiel might have lived to witness this day.

Three days later when, on motion of the Honorable Thomas J. Durant, she was admitted to the United States Court of Claims, her triumph was complete. It was in this court, on the lower floor of the Freedman's Bank Building on Pennsylvania Avenue opposite the Treasury Building, that Belva was to win some of her most important cases. It was the only court in which a citizen could prosecute his claim against the government. Claims for salvage, royalties, soldiers' benefits, and Southern war claims were all heard before the five justices of the court, one of whom was Belva's former opponent Judge Nott, who had said, "A woman is without legal capacity to take the office of attorney."

Letters and wires came in from all over the country offering congratulations. Still there was criticism in many newspapers. Editors voiced the view that it was unseemly for a lady to compete with men in the courts, "where the words of aggressive argument should be kept from female ears." Cartoonists pictured Belva curtsying coyly before the Supreme Court judges.

When walking down the street one day, a well-dressed man waved a clenched fist in her face. "You are destroying the sanctity of the family."

Belva returned to her home visibly shaken. Before retiring she decided to visit with Lura. She depended more than ever for solace and companionship on her daughter now that Ezekiel was gone.

"Have I gone too far, Lura? Are people really so opposed to my views, to my principles?"

"Mother, I'm surprised you should have any doubts. Their attacks only show that they fear the success you've already won. You should never give up the fight for women's suffrage."

Belva put her arm around Lura's shoulder. "You've eased my troubles so many times. People expect me to have strength. I've faltered so often."

Lura shook her head. "So seldom, Mother."

Women's rights was not the only cause Belva fought for. Somehow during her long day she found time to serve as secretary of the financial committee of the Universal Peace Union, to appear before Congressional committees to urge legislation specifying the rights of minority groups, and to work for the appointment of a matron for the District jail, a simple request that had been denied other workers for penal reform.

Belva Lockwood broke still another traditional prejudice. On February 20, 1880, she again stood before Chief Justice Morrison Waite in the chambers of the Supreme Court of the United States, this time with a motion that would admit Mr. Samuel Lowery to practice before the court. History was being made. Mr. Lowery was a black, a Southern black.

He was a man of many interests and accomplishments. He was a clergyman who had served as a chaplain during the Civil War, and he was an imaginative experimenter trying various ways to increase agricultural production in the South, even attempting to introduce the science of silk culture to the United States. Mr. Lowery was principal of the Huntsville Industrial University of Alabama, an institution that was doing an excellent job training blacks for occupations that would raise their standard of living. Yet he, too, found that he needed the backing of the law to help fight prejudice. Belva welcomed the opportunity to use her own legal battering rams to break down barriers for others. Through her insistence and continual letter-writing campaign, backed up with legal briefs, Mr. Lowery was accepted before the highest court of the land.

Since Belva had earned her law diploma, other young women had followed her example—to be sure only a few, but an encouraging sign. Belva's practice was large. She finally decided to take on two other women lawyers as partners. One was her friend Mrs. Marilla Ricker, who had become known as "the prisoners' friend" and also as one who "fears neither God, man, nor the devil because she does not particularly believe in any of them." The third of the "three graces," as the Washington newspapers delighted in calling the trio, was Mrs. Lavina Dundore. Now that Lura needed more time with her family, Belva hired Miss Tillie Sadler, a young woman typewriter, as stenographers were called in that day. Together they proved what Belva had always contended, that brilliance and efficiency were attributes of both sexes. Now she was free to take on even more commitments.

Belva was the logical choice to represent the women of Washington at the Republican National Convention in Chicago in 1880. She had drafted a proposal that the platform committee incorporate a plank guaranteeing women's suffrage. Belva had no illusions that it would be accepted without a fight, but if battle were necessary, fight she would. Too many elected officials feared female enthusiasm for reform.

The convention was held in the hall of the fabulous new Palmer House, the hotel that had just been rebuilt after the disastrous Chicago fire. It was the first entirely fireproof structure of its size ever built; there was not a wooden partition in the entire building. The handsome staircase in the main lobby was made of precious marble imported from Europe. An amazing elevator took Belva to the fifth floor to explore the tropical roof garden under glass. Lura would surely think she'd invented these stories, she thought. Her own room, and there were some seven hundred others under this roof, had its own marble tub in a separate dressing room. Belva shook her head at such luxury. She twirled around the room like a little girl, touching the fine fabric of the draperies, smiling at herself in the gilt-framed mirror. Her up-the-ladder room in Niagara County was never like this.

Chicago was an amazing city of almost 700,000 people. Hundreds of new buildings were under construction. The Board of Trade building climbed 172 feet into the sky. Everywhere a trestle of iron girders framed the skyline. This new building technique made it possible for the first time for architects to design structures that reached such dizzy heights. She wished she had more time to explore the city, but there was other excitement, meeting some of the most important political leaders of the country.

Yet she was disheartened by the petty arguments and haggling for favors that preceded the selection of candidates. On the first ballot ex-President Grant led by a slim margin, 304 votes to 284 for James G. Blaine, who had served as Speaker of the House and had a strong following himself.

The convention hall of the Palmer House could accommodate some two thousand people, but almost twice that number edged their way into the stifling hot auditorium. Seats had been jammed to the walls. Hour after hour Belva listened to the harangue of speakers, the clapping, booing, whistling, and stamping of delegates, and the thumping, blaring noise of marching bands. Even when she retired to her room she could not shut out the din.

She was not the only one worn out from lack of sleep. Tempers stretched thin. As hour after hour passed and ballot after ballot was taken, nothing was being accomplished. A few votes shifted from side to side, but it became evident that neither man could win a majority.

Belva was far from the private sessions that finally broke the deadlock. The almost unknown name of James Garfield of Ohio was proposed as a compromise candidate, and finally on the thirty-fifth ballot a weary crowd cheered their nominee. Chester Arthur of Vermont was quickly chosen to be his running mate for Vice President.

Now the real work of the convention could get under way, but by this time many delegates had chosen to go home, and the party leaders had their way in the dictation of policy.

On the afternoon of June 2, the platform committee convened to plan the strategy and issues of the coming campaign. Mrs. Lockwood rose to read the statement of purpose of the Woman Suffrage Association. "Seventy-six delegates from local and national suffrage associations representing every section of the United States ask you, no demand, that you place the following plank in your platform.

" 'Resolved that we pledge ourselves to secure to women the exercise of their right to vote.' Our party must stand for progress and justice. This vital issue will rouse the enthusiasm and trust of the nation's voters. You will not only win support from the electorate, but most important of all, you will know that you have taken the first step to right an intolerable wrong."

Her words were delivered dramatically, but when she sat down, there was only a smattering of polite applause. Belva realized at once that she had failed to win support for her cause. She stayed for the rest of the morning's program, then returned to her hotel and packed her bag. She felt discouraged and bone weary. She wished Ezekiel could be with her to help her gain some perspective on the events. What more could she have done? But how foolish to waste her time fretting. Tired or not, there was one more thing she wanted to do. Before boarding the train for Washington, she decided to spend an hour or two touring the Interstate Exposition Hall. She had read that many new mechanical marvels would be on display. DeForest would surely want to hear about these inventions, and Belva herself had always been interested in science.

All sorts of gadgets were shown, even one that could cook food with electricity, but what excited her most was a simple means of transportation that could be most useful to her.

"That is just what I need. I'll have one shipped to Washington."

Fourteen

It was a memorable day when she tried out her new purchase. Judges Henrich and Balch were hurrying on foot to their offices on F Street. They stopped at a street corner while a parade of assorted vehicles passed by. Drivers flicked whips. Horses snorted. Henrich saw a break in traffic and lunged ahead, almost to be run down by a strange vehicle whose driver was noisily clanging a bell of warning. He jumped back to avoid a collision, but as he looked up in annoyance, his mouth dropped open in astonishment.

Judge Balch, who had remained on the sidewalk, chuckled at his friend's surprise. Then with a mock show of dignity, he removed his hat with a flourish, bowed slightly, and called out his greeting to the passing speedster. "Good day, Mrs. Lockwood."

"Just who was that and what was that?" Henrich demanded.

"That, my friend, is our colleague, lady lawyer Lockwood, and that contrivance which almost ran you down looks very much like a tricycle, I believe they call it, which I saw pictured in one of the journals."

Judge Henrich shook his head in disbelief. "What will she try next?"

Robert Balch grinned. "I shudder to think, but I vow it will be the unexpected."

That was an excellent prediction, but Belva never once planned her actions to create a sensational effect. Lura criticized the tricycle. "Mother, it isn't ladylike to dash around Washington so. People will talk."

Belva had answered, "I have frequently been talked about, and I surely won't give up this convenience. I can now plan a tight schedule without having to wait for hired cabs."

She continued to be seen everywhere in Washington on her famous tricycle. A specially designed dashboard kept her skirts modestly in place. Her plumed hats were secured firmly on her pile of brown curls with dagger-like hatpins, and she maintained all the dignity that might be expected of a queen riding in her royal coach.

And her schedule was busier than ever. However, she was willing to drop everything if her latest petition were accepted. She had persuaded the Honorable Albert C. Ridder to endorse her appointment as minister to Brazil. She had always been interested in fostering friendship between the Americas, but some who heard of her latest request accused her of unbridled ambition and of trying to keep her name in the public eye. Although there was no doubt that she had ambition, her drive was spurred by her desire to break down every barrier to her sex, to prove that "women can do that too."

Riddle had promised to help her attain a post in the foreign service, and even President Garfield had said he was in favor of such an appointment. But on July 2, just four months after his inauguration, an assassin's bullet ended the President's life. Chester Arthur took over a government in need of reform. The Republican party found itself waging a defensive political battle for the first time in twenty years. It was not the time to come to the aid of women's rights, not Mrs. Lockwood's rights, just yet.

Belva continued to divide her six-day work week between her law office and court. But by the time the next Republican convention met in 1884, she was prepared to marshal her forces for yet another battle for women's suffrage. Again she packed her bags for the convention city of Chicago.

Now that she was a veteran of one national political meeting, she felt she knew how to go about her campaign. She had discovered that opinion could be swayed more easily talking to individuals rather than a mass audience. She would seek out leaders even when debates were being waged on the floor. Only a few could really hear what was going on during the long droning speeches that many lesser politicians were sure to give. The real business often took place furtively, with blocks of votes being jumped from one camp to another, much like a chess match. Belva did not approve of such closed dealings, but she was wise enough to know that she would not be able to change the system. In fact, it would be to her advantage to use these same tactics.

Henry Ward Beecher was one of the first men she approached. She had admired his address before the convention demanding an end to the odious form of patronage, graft, and corruption that had entered the last election. Mr. Beecher listened to Belva attentively and assured her of his own private support, but he said there was little he could do for her cause until other matters of business were settled.

The delegates took only four ballots to determine that James G. Blaine, who had served as Secretary of State during the last administration, was to be their candidate. Now Belva hoped the time had come for Beecher and others to voice their support of a universal suffrage plank in the platform. She was bitterly disappointed when the resolutions committee again refused to consider any proposal guaranteeing equal rights for women.

Mrs. Lockwood was not the only feminist who received rough treatment during the hearings. Miss Francis Willard was booed from the platform when she submitted a petition signed by twenty thousand people. Belva returned to Washington discouraged and disgusted. How could she support a party led by men with such bigoted views? She sat down at her desk and put her thoughts into words.

"Even if women in the United States are not permitted to vote, there is no law against their being voted for and, if elected, filling the highest office in the gift of the people.

"Why not nominate women for important places? Is not Victoria Empress of India? Is not history full of precedents of women rulers? Have we not among our own countrywomen persons of as much talent and ability?

"The Republican party, claiming to be the party of progress, has little but insult for women when they appear before its conventions. It is time we had our own party, our own platform and our own nominees.

"We shall never have equal rights until we take them, nor respect until we command it. If we act up to our convictions of justice and equal right, we will not far go wrong."

What paper would dare print that? She immediately thought of Marietta Stow, editor of the *Woman's Herald of Industry*. Belva did not exactly approve of Mrs. Stow's flamboyant style of life. Mrs. Stow designed her own clothing, which she called a "Triple S Costume." It consisted of a man's pair of trousers over which she wore a kilt skirt. She espoused many strange causes, claiming to cure illness with a new type of electric shock treatment, and she had recently founded a dietetic cult, preaching that one should eat only cold food. But Mrs. Stow was an indefatigable worker for the Equal Rights Party. For this, Belva counted Mrs. Stow one of her friends and supporters.

The letter was duly mailed to Mrs. Stow in California and then forgotten because of Belva's heavy work load. Several weeks later she received a reply from her forgotten letter. Belva noted the California postmark on the envelope and wondered if Mrs. Stow had ever bothered to publish her comments. Belva read and reread the letter before quite believing the words.

"We have the honor to congratulate you as the first woman ever nominated for the office of President of the United States." *

Was someone playing a joke on her?

The offer was far from a joke. Her letter had been pub-

* Victoria Woodhull was nominated for President in 1872, but her party disintegrated before the election. Thus Belva Lockwood is the first woman formally to run for the office.

134

lished, and it had been read and applauded at the California meeting of the Equal Rights party. Immediately her name was placed in nomination as one who would "bring no blush or barnacles of youthful or mature wild oats sowing into the White House to smirch the Nation's escutcheon. . . . She sits at the gate of the temple and the Nation's heart beats in unison with the Equal Rights party."

Mrs. Stow added her own words. "We await your letter of acceptance with breathless interest."

Belva had no illusions that she would be able to attract sufficient support to win the presidency, but surely her efforts would bring attention to the issue of women's suffrage. Again there would be criticism that she was asking for notoriety. She had been able to endure the accusation before, why not now? She consulted with Lura and her law partners, Mrs. Dundore and Mrs. Ricker. All three agreed that she must not refuse the opportunity offered.

"I'm so proud, Mother," said Lura.

Belva composed her answer carefully, for in her acceptance she formulated her platform and campaign strategy. If her backers did not agree with all her policies, she promised to withdraw her name as a nominee. She would oppose "wholesale monopoly of the judiciary of the country by male voters" and would "seek to secure a fair distribution of the public offices to women as well as men." If a vacancy occurred on the United States Supreme Court, she promised she would appoint a competent woman for that post. "We pledge ourselves, if elected, with power so far as in us lies, to do justice to every class of citizens without distinction of color, sex or nationality."

She would "protect and foster American industries" and at the same time foster the extension of commerce with foreign countries. She would provide additional benefits for widows and orphans. She was in favor of temperance laws, and she pledged to fight for full citizenship rights for the American Indian.

Who could possibly attack such lofty goals? Just about everyone it seemed, but she was ready to fight. As the *Woman's Herald of Industry* recorded, she had "climbed Capitol Hill to face the bearded lions in their marble stronghold."

Mrs. Lockwood did not suffer from lack of newspaper coverage, but reporters and cartoonists made fun of her at every opportunity. She was called a Portia with no thought of what her proposals would do in wrecking the nation's economy and destroying the family home. If women were treated as equals, they'd have the right to leave dishes in the sink and their poor waifs untended on the street. Men were uncomfortably concerned about how the "little woman" would react in the privacy of the polling booth.

In a serious vein, Belva argued that "women have always been the chief sufferers of bad legislation, and being the weaker sex physically, it is harder for them to acquire a fortune, the more need of the legal knowledge of how to keep it. Give them this education."

Belva was bitterly disappointed that Susan Anthony and Elizabeth Stanton disapproved of her actions. They felt that the fight for women's rights should not be diluted in a hopeless campaign for national office. She should work within the framework of one of the major parties. She was blamed for bringing ridicule and contempt to the cause of woman's suffrage at a time when it was beginning to command respect. She was also accused of running for office for the sole purpose of increasing her law practice through the publicity she received in the press.

Belva of course denied this claim. She argued that whatever votes she won could be marked as an entering wedge in the fight for women's suffrage. A lesser woman would surely have given up, but Belva was not without some friends.

Miss Anthony and Mrs. Stanton made the point that Belva's name had been placed in nomination by only a small group of radical friends from the West, surely not enough support for her to assume a national candidacy. It was obviously true, and to rectify the situation, a group of women from Washington, D.C., decided on a grand ratification meeting. As no one in the District of Columbia had a vote, an electoral ticket was prepared for Maryland. Mrs. Amanda Best, an active suffragist, offered her home in Prince George County, Maryland, for the meeting.

This would be Belva's first appearance since having been proposed as a candidate. Although she would be among friends, the press would surely be covering the event. She was rarely nervous on a speakers' platform, but now she was worried. She tried to anticipate the sorts of questions she'd be asked. It would be a hard test.

She dressed carefully in a new blue silk suit with a matching hat. The ladies and a few interested and/or curious gentlemen from Washington had reserved several cars on the commuter train for the trip to Maryland. Belva was surprised so many had made reservations. She stood on the station platform with her daughter and son-in-law while strangers and friends alike came up to offer their congratulations.

A young man with a pad and pencil pushed through the crowd and shouted his question. "Just how do you plan to decorate the White House, Mrs. Lockwood?" His grin was insolent.

Belva frowned. "I am not promising my supporters success in this campaign, but I believe by our statement of policy we may influence others to incorporate some of these reforms in their own platforms."

The young man's grin faded as he sensed the sincerity of the woman standing before him. By the end of the day many skeptics had been won over and original believers had reaffirmed their loyalty. Mrs. Belva Ann Lockwood could now officially claim the nomination. Mrs. Marietta Stow was chosen to run for the vice presidency, as she could cover the western states in a series of speaking engagements.

Both women immediately embarked on a killing schedule of appearances. Belva spoke before dozens of groups in New York, Philadelphia, Cincinnati, Cleveland, and Chicago. The candidates marshaled their forces to work for electoral tickets in every state where any known organization favored the women's suffrage movement. Mrs. Ricker was asked to represent the state of New Hampshire; Cynthia Leonard, New York State; Mrs. Best, Maryland; Leila Robinson, Oregon; and Clara Foltz, California.

Belva's reform ticket also attracted some masculine support. The Lockwood Club of Rahway, New Jersey, an all-male organization, joined the bandwagon by parading the streets in poke bonnets and flourishing banners with appropriate slogans, "Peace and Liberty," "Prosperity and Equal Rights." The serious intent of most of her supporters was harmed by a few exuberant well-wishers who formed Mother Hubbard Clubs, dressing in women's clothing and parading through the streets of Terre Haute, Indiana, and yet some of these merrymakers eventually did make it to the polls to give her a vote of confidence.

The Broom Brigades of New York carried cleaning equipment and promised to sweep the city clean of corruption. The campaign was a combination of tongue-in-cheek merriment and sincere dedication to reform. Obviously the press considered the former escapades of the jokesters more interesting copy for their readers.

Yet Belva's words reached the editorial pages of dozens of papers. "Who are the people of the United States? . . . Are the women persons? Are they citizens? May they be freeholders, and can they sue and be sued? We are governed without our own consent. . . . The full-fledged American woman stands before you today ready for the workshop, ready for the pulpit, the forum, or the political arena, demanding equal political rights under the Constitution and equal rights under the law."

From Cleveland's Opera House to New York's Academy of Music she strode the speakers' platform. "Our chief enemy is public apathy," she said. "Too many women have not enough time left in the day for effective indignation against their status."

In spite of Belva's dramatic oratory, Grover Cleveland was elected to the Presidency over his Republican opponent, James G. Blaine, but Mrs. Lockwood and her running mate, Mrs. Stow, had polled 6,161 votes from an all-male electorate.

New York	1,346
New Hampshire	379
Michigan	374
Illinois	1,008
Maryland	318
California	734
Indiana	2,002

Belva knew they had won votes in other states, but when complaints were filed, the election judges shrugged their shoulders and said the count had been so small that it was not necessary to tabulate it. This was certainly not the legal way to hold an election, and Belva vowed that she would conduct an investigation in every state not announcing a vote for the Equal Rights party. The magnitude and cost of the threat was prohibitive. She had to content herself with knowing that a precedent had been set and the prestige of women had been enhanced.

"The fact that a woman actually ran for President," she said to Lura, "will give men something to think about for years to come."

And that it did.

Fifteen

The speaking tour ended. It had been a trying schedule, but Belva had enjoyed every minute of it. She loved an audience. It was always a challenge to sway opinions, to fight for a cause. What could she tackle now that would not be an anticlimax to her presidential campaign?

She readily found her cause and perhaps her most important mission in life, peace on earth. What more noble aim? This was not exactly a new page in Belva's journal. She had attended many meetings of local pacifist groups, but her first important action was a legal maneuver. In 1885 she wrote and presented to Congress the first bill ever to be considered advocating an international court to preserve world peace.

"If nations could only depend upon fair and impartial judgments in a world court of law, they would abandon the senseless, savage practice of war," she said.

The men of Congress nodded their heads wisely, sympathetically, but declined to commit themselves to international entanglements at a time when European power politics was a mass of intrigue. Yet during the same year the State Department appointed Mrs. Lockwood delegate to the Congress of Charities, the first world pacifist congress, to be held in Geneva, Switzerland.

Belva hesitated to accept the appointment. "I've spent so much time away from my law practice because of my campaign that I have dropped too many other responsibilities. I'd be leaving a full load of work at the office."

"Mother, you're joking," Lura said.

"I've hired two more women clerks, the Harrison sisters," Belva continued the debate with herself, "but still I wonder if I should go."

"I never thought you would hesitate for a moment," Lura continued. "What more important service could you render than to represent the United States in world plans for peace and foreign aid?"

Belva smiled. "I've always dreamed of traveling abroad, but I am afraid I am getting too old."

"You're younger than women half your age," Lura argued.

It was true. Belva had an amazing store of energy and certainly a youthful appearance for her age. In her childhood she had despaired of her pinched features and her skinny frame. Now in her fifties, the tautness of her skin kept wrinkles from admitting years, and her slim figure and tiny waist were features to be proud of. Belva had a new dress made for the trip. She dreamed of owning a Paris gown, but she knew she'd probably be too busy for much shopping or sightseeing.

Belva traveled by train to New York and hired a cab to drive her to the dock at the waterfront. When she looked up at the huge ocean liner, she was as excited as a child, almost as excited, she said to herself, as on that first trip on the canal boat.

The crossing took a week. Belva marveled at the luxury of

the ship, the ballroom-size dining room, the attentive service of the crew. She spent hours in her steamer chair enjoying the sun and fresh air, relaxing for the first time in weeks. She was a bit embarrassed that her face had taken on a ruddy tan by the time they were ready to land.

Her rest soon ended. Meetings kept her busy from morning to night. Belva was seated next to Frederic Passy, the Frenchman who had founded the League International of Paris, afterwards known as the French Society of Arbitration between Nations. He was delighted and surprised to meet a lady lawyer who had the courage and vision to lobby for an international court of law. Belva was asked to read her proposal, which had received little serious consideration in her own country.

Now the applause was deafening. Strangers came up to congratulate her, asking for copies of her legal memorandum that could be proposed in their own countries. Belva felt satisfaction at last that she was not alone in her commitment to a world court. She vowed that she would never give up the fight to see this legislation passed in the United States.

On the sea voyage home she spent most of her time drafting letters to influential friends and to newspapers that might be counted on to print her words of urgency to establish an arbitrational committee. Back in Washington she focused all of her energy toward this one project.

In 1886 she went abroad again as the official representative to the Second International Peace Conference, this time being held in Budapest, Hungary. The Reverend Amanda Dayo, a minister of the Universalist Church of New York, went with her. It was pleasant to have a friend with whom she could share travel experiences and heated discussions on women's rights. Amanda Dayo had earned her own reputation as a crusader in this field.

On this trip Belva allowed herself the luxury of being a tourist, exploring the city. Hungary was celebrating its one hundredth anniversary of independence from the Turks. Budapest was spruced for tourists. Guided tours by carriage were arranged for all delegates.

"Time seems to have stopped here. Their whole city is a museum," Belva said to Amanda. "When I think that some of these weathered buildings were old before the Pilgrims landed in our own country. . . . And see how beautifully Eastern and Western cultures have fused to make an original style so very much its own. I'm an old woman, Amanda, but I am going to spend more time traveling. The world is such a huge place, and every place I visit is so surprisingly different." She laughed. "It shows I'm not a very cosmopolitan citizen of the world after all when I'm just discovering this simple truth."

But Belva put off traveling for more than a year. She was first of all a joiner and crusader. She was elected an officer of the District Federation of Women's Clubs, the Woman's National Press Association, and a dozen organizations sponsoring peace and suffrage for all. She had become a well-known celebrity. Her words were often quoted. She was always in demand as a speaker, and she rarely refused.

Once more in 1886 she was nominated for the Presidency of the United States, this time by the Equal Rights party of Iowa. Alfred Love of the Universal Peace Union was her running mate. Mr. Love himself added much to the prestige of the ticket. He was the son of a well-to-do Quaker family of Philadelphia. At the time of the Civil War he had argued bitterly to end the war by passive resistance. He not only refused to fight in the war, but he would not pay any military tax that would support the war. He also refused in his woolen textile business to handle any army orders. It meant a loss of the family business, but Love would not compromise his nonviolent philosophy. After the war was over, he formed the Universal Peace Union. He was a man respected and admired even by those who could not endorse all of his radical policies.

This time the circus antics were eliminated, although campaign buttons were distributed everywhere with the words "Love our Lockwood" framing a portrait of the lady politician. The public was more willing to picture the candidates as dignified, sincere reformers.

Again Belva hit the campaign trail. She flourished a banner inscribed on one side with the word "Peace" and on the other "Women's Rights." In all kinds of weather she traveled from city to city. More than once she was forced to sleep in a train station waiting room, but she was never one to complain and always seemed to appear on a platform fresh, energetic, and full of enthusiasm for what she believed was right, for what she believed the public would some day vote into being.

In a close election General Benjamin Harrison defeated Grover Cleveland. Neither party had been so bold as to endorse Belva's platform, but again the public was made aware of her program. She was steadily gaining support for these ideas.

In 1890 a son was born to Lura Ormes, a son who was later to become the closest friend and confidant of his grandmother. Her granddaughters were dear to her, but Belva shamelessly spoiled her grandson and showered him with love and small gifts. Belva's home life centered around her daughter's family. "I always did want a son. This should keep me closer to the hearth fire," she said.

Lura smiled. "Mother, I'll know something is wrong if you become too attached to this place. I'm sure right now you have plans for a trip. Tell me honestly, where are you going?"

Belva nodded. "I do hope to travel some more. I thought I'd attend the International Peace Congress this summer."

Lura laughed. "We'll keep the home fires going while you see the world."

Again Belva crossed the ocean. She had given up hope of establishing an international court of law for the time being, but she intended to ask for a practical treaty of faith between nations. She read her paper on disarmament to a packed audience in London's Westminster Hall.

"No one can claim to be called Christian who gives money for the building of warships and arsenals."

Delegates from twenty nations had assembled to discuss not only moral arguments for peaceful commitment, but also practical ways to implement these decisions. They discussed the massacres in Turkey and the Armenian internal conflict. Every year there were new outbreaks of war. In many cases the peace conferences did help bring mediation and prevented the spread of a full-scale war.

"Our accomplishments may seem small," she wrote to Lura, "when they are reported on the back pages of newspapers, but we have prevented, more than once, a bloody war headline."

Mrs. Lockwood was not only a speaker but an attentive listener as well. Never did she feel that her education was over. Before returning home from this conference, she stayed on to enroll in a series of lectures at Oxford University on political science. "I have so much to learn," she wrote.

And so much to do, she might have added. Alfred Love persuaded her to embark on a research job that was to take hours of her time and energy. She compiled a "List of Treaties and Arbitrations Concluded between the United States and Foreign Powers." It was hoped that it would prove to the American people that diplomacy, not military might, had been able to solve problems that might otherwise have flared into war.

In addition to her committee work, she handled every type of legal matter, but the most important case of her career, the defense of the Cherokee Indians against the United States government, was still to be heard in court.

Sixteen

Early in her practice Belva had met Mr. Jim Taylor, a Cherokee Indian from North Carolina. She had successfully collected some money due him. Now he turned to her for help for all of his people. It involved a sum of money for land purchased by the United States government.

The original terms of the claim had been agreed upon in 1835 with the Treaty of New Echota, but it was an agreement made with only a few of the Cherokee leaders.

The ancestral homeland of the Cherokees was in the rich and rolling foothills and heights of the Great Smoky range. Their hunting grounds sprawled across what is now North Carolina, Tennessee, Alabama, and Georgia. In the early 1800s it was crowded with all kinds of game, but the Indians did not depend on their hunting skills alone for food. Even before the white man came to their country, they had plowed fields and planted corn and grain. Since white neighbors edged into their land, they had adopted many of the white man's ways. They were the first Indian nation to translate their spoken words to a written language. They set up schools for their children and taught them what was best of both cultures. The Indians prospered. Most of them built log houses like their white neighbors. They learned of other crops to plant, and they worked hard on their farms.

As settlers pushed the frontier farther and farther west, they looked with envy at the rich, cleared lands of the Cherokees. In 1830, the year Belva was born, the United States Congress passed the Indian Removal Bill, designed to relocate all Indian tribes west of the Mississippi. The Indians were told of a rich promised land where they could settle their people without fear of crowding by the whites. Some of the Indians took these words as truth and moved their families to land that is now in the state of Oklahoma. Most stayed on.

Finally agents representing the United States government wrote the Treaty of New Echota, exchanging the Cherokee eastern acres for lands in the new Indian territory of Oklahoma. When the treaty was presented to the Indians, only 79 of the nearly 16,000 Cherokees signed the document, yet the United States considered it a binding agreement.

In 1838 troops were sent to Cherokee country to enforce the fraudulent treaty. Fourteen thousand Indians were gathered together and marched westward. The winter was bad. Food was scarce. Four thousand died on the march, which has since been called the "Trail of Tears." Yet there were some Cherokees, more than a thousand, who escaped deportation by living as fugitives in the Great Smoky Mountains. They did not share in the payment for the land. More than a generation passed before they sought help in the form of a new treaty that would let them stay legally on the land they had worked for so many years.

A new treaty was signed in 1891. Mrs. Lockwood's help was sought to collect the money owed these families. The government did not question the purchase price originally agreed upon. The court action was started to collect the interest on the yet unpaid principal, which over the last sixty years now amounted to far more than the original sum.

Not only weeks, but years went into the preparation of this case. It was the climax of Belva's career. She was charged with the defense of between three and four thousand families, or from twelve to fifteen thousand people. Where some families had traveled to the West and others remained in the East, their claims had to be divided and subdivided in a masterful attempt to mete out delayed justice.

Belva traveled to Muskogee in the Indian Territory to file briefs and motions and petitions for some seventeen separate land cases. She also had to review every written document involving the role of the United States government in negotiating treaties and agreements governing the Cherokee nation over not one, but two generations. The amount of research involved was overwhelming.

She had tried to manage without asking Lura's help, but now that she was swamped with past-due correspondence on other matters, Lura volunteered to spend mornings at the office. While others might have been able to take over the work, no one seemed quite able to anticipate Belva's thoughts and wishes as Lura did, and no one quite equaled Lura's dependability. When Lura sent word one day that she was unable to help because of illness, Belva knew that it must be serious. She hurried to her daughter's home and was shocked to see how pale she looked and how frail.

"Lura dear, you must rest now and build your strength. I've been working you way too hard."

Lura smiled weakly. "You've been twice as busy as I have, Mother. If you could share just a bit of your own energy, I'd be out of this bed in no time."

"But I don't have a husband and children who require my attention either."

Lura turned her face toward the wall to keep her mother from seeing the tears that filled her eyes. "Who will take care of little Forest? The girls are in school, but there's no place for a four-year-old."

"Why, he'll come to stay with his grandmother until you are well, dear. Don't worry."

"But you are so busy, Mother."

"Never too busy for Forest. I'm truly exhausted myself. I'm going to take a few days away from the office. We'll pack a picnic and maybe even find an apple tree to climb."

Lura smiled, but her head slumped weakly against her pillow. Belva left the room quietly. She had a long worried conference with her son-in-law. Yes, the doctor had been called, but he had no diagnosis as to what was wrong and what might help. The weakness had come upon her very suddenly.

"I'm taking Forest with me, but I'll be back tomorrow," she said.

Lura died that night before she returned. Belva had lived through tragedy before. She had lost two husbands, a sister, and a daughter, but Lura's sudden death was the hardest of all to bear. Belva was grief-stricken. DeForest himself sat in stunned silence. Neither husband nor mother could console one another. Their sorrow was so intense that words could not release their grief.

It was little Forest who brought Belva back to her senses. That evening he tugged impatiently at his grandmother's hand. "I'm hungry, aren't you?"

Belva picked him up and hugged him to her closely. "I'm sorry, Forest. Of course you are hungry. I'll get supper now. Forest, you will stay with me, won't you?"

"For always?"

"We will ask your father. Would you like that?"

He hesitated only a moment and nodded.

The day after the funeral Belva spoke to her son-in-law. "Do you think you could lend me your son for a while?"

DeForest did not seem surprised. "I know he would be happy with you. He has already asked me if he could pack his suitcase. His sister Rhoda has also offered to help, but I know she had her heart set on being away at school this fall, and with Inez just married, I had thought I had best find a house-keeper to care for him."

"Please DeForest, I do need him."

"But Mother Lockwood, a four-year-old grandson may be more than you want to manage."

"Let me try. We will be near you. We can share our time with him," Belva pleaded.

Forest happily moved in with his grandmother for a trial visit. It was a visit that lasted many years. Belva recognized that she would never be able to live a solitary life confined to home, but she had always been able to give of herself completely during the time she spent with her loved ones. It was strange to see little Forest perched on a chair in his grandmother's office or riding on Belva's lap while she pedaled her tricycle around Washington. A nursemaid was hired but used only on occasions. It was hard to find apple trees for climbing in the city of Washington, but they picnicked in the parks and climbed the newly dedicated Washington Monument together.

Forest was not always a quiet little boy. He loved to explore, and more than once his adventures caused Belva anxiety. He had accompanied Belva one day to the office of Indian Affairs, where she was consulting an agent about a legal problem involving the complicated inheritance procedure. Belva had been deeply engrossed in some records for almost an hour when she suddenly realized that Forest was missing.

She began a search room by room of the offices down the long corridor. He was nowhere in sight. Could he have gone out to the street? Belva was about to rush outdoors when she heard her name being called. "Mrs. Lockwood, I believe you can help me identify a member of this tribe."

One of the office workers was holding the hand of a belligerent young boy wearing a full-feathered war bonnet. In one of the rooms there was a display of Indian finery, handsome bead and quill work. Young Forest had dragged down the finest trophy and had set up his own tepee under a desk. There was laughter all around, but not from grandmother.

"I hope he has not damaged this property," she said.

"No, I believe it was retrieved before a war party arrived." The man laughed again.

"I will see that he is punished," said Belva.

Forest was banished to his room for the rest of the day, but Belva relented by dinnertime, and the two shared supper by the fireplace.

Belva carried on a limited law practice, but she canceled most of her speaking engagements. She asked Jim Taylor to give her more time to bring the Cherokee case to trial. She did not feel that she could travel now, not with young Forest. She was tired and she was angry. Her attention was drawn to world headlines. There seemed no hope for peace in the world. She watched as the United States was being drawn into war with Spain. She read the fiery editorials published by two of the country's leading news editors, William Randolph Hearst and Joseph Pulitzer. They continued to print stories of cruel atrocities supposedly inflicted by the ruling Spanish generals on the revolting Cubans. The public sympathized with the Cuban underdogs. Much pressure was brought to bear on President Cleveland to become involved in the conflict in the name of upholding justice.

Belva broke her silence briefly, taking to the speakers' platform again to try to quash the militant tide of sentiment. "If justice is to be done, it must be decided in a world court, not on a bloody battlefield. There judgment, not emotion, will rule the decision."

A few did listen to her words, but on February 15, 1898, the battleship *Maine* exploded while in the harbor of Havana. The Spanish were blamed. President McKinley, who was then in office, demanded that the Spanish withdraw from Cuba. They refused, and war was declared.

Belva was sick with disappointment that the world had not listened to reason. She even blamed herself for her temporary retirement. It was then she decided she could not afford to relax her efforts for world-wide arbitration. If one speech could influence but one person, it was worthwhile.

Belva returned to her work with renewed energy. The war was soon over, not because of the efforts of the pacifist faction of government, but because of the superior military power of the United States' armed forces. Again she began to write letters to heads of states all over the world. Spending more time in her office brought her attention around to her own law practice. Again she turned her energy to renewed work for the Cherokee Indians. She planned to increase her demands on their behalf. Who should pay for the relocation of the whole tribe?

Belva wrote, "To make them pay for their removal from homes which they did not wish to leave, to a country to which they did not wish to go, was a monstrous abuse of the obscure provisions of a treaty which they had not read, which they had not signed, and to which they had not in fact been parties."

The case was to be tried before Judge Charles C. Nott, the very judge who had opposed her practice before this same United States Court of Claims, who had said thirty-three years before, "A woman is without legal capacity to take the office of attorney."

Belva felt a very personal challenge in the preparation of the case, yet her main incentive was her conviction that the Indians had been treated inhumanely. Though a monetary settlement could never repay them for the hardships they had endured, it would set a precedent for the handling of future Indian affairs.

Six more years of research and negotiation took place before the final case was judged. She pleaded her case well. On March 20, 1905, a decision was reached. Chief Justice Nott delivered his opinion.

"The Cherokee Nation has parted with the land and has lost the time within which it might have appealed to the courts. . . . The United States are placed in a position of having broken and evaded the letter and spirit of their agreement." Nevertheless, he refused to allow the full interest claimed by Attorney Lockwood.

Belva had no intention of giving up. The money was due the Indians. She would not permit the judge to admit a wrong and then not right the injustice. She appealed the case to the Supreme Court of the United States. Again she rose to plead the case eloquently, passionately, backed with the facts and figures of legal precedents. The chief justice had cautioned her to limit her summation to ten minutes, but as she tore apart the defense, logically, meticulously, the nine judges listened for forty-five minutes. It was later said that she had made "the most eloquent argument any attorney had made before that court."

Questions and answers were thrown and parried. Why, she was asked, did she claim interest on the settlement when the government was willing to honor a most generous settlement? Her answer was short and logical, "Because it was an interest-bearing fund."

Chief Justice Fuller finally delivered the decision. "We agree that the United States are liable. . . . The monies should be paid directly to the equitable owners."

Mrs. Lockwood had won $5,000,000 for the Cherokee Indians, about $4,000,000 of which was accumulated interest on the amount promised by the original treaty. The newspapers reported that she had won "the most important case, as far as amount of money is involved, which has ever been brought before the United States Court of Claims and the United States Supreme Court."

Her share of the fees was approximately $50,000, an enormous amount in those days, but she had earned every penny of that, proving that a woman's, at least this woman's, determination and intelligence most probably surpassed that of most of her male colleagues. Under any set of standards she could be regarded as a "success" and a shining example, vindicating the power of woman to take a high place in the legal profession.

She was warmly congratulated by friends and foes alike, but she was proudest that her grandson could say, "Grandma, you were great." He had been sitting in the gallery listening to the entire proceedings.

At seventy-five she *was* certainly great. Everyone marveled at her stamina and asked when she planned to retire. "While my health permits, I will continue to appear in court," was her reply.

In 1912, when she was eighty-one, she could write, "I have three heavy law cases on hand, one in the Court of Claims . . . and the others in the District Supreme Court . . . and am tried with details not settled."

It was not until her eighty-third birthday that she finally announced that she planned to retire from her active law practice to devote her time exclusively to public issues. She had always been a practical woman in matters of finance, but because of her generosity to sympathetic causes and individuals whom she felt deserving, she found herself with very little income at the end of her life. She had invested heavily in a building project, housing for the needy in the Washington area. The builder had run out of funds. She had arranged to take on a second mortgage for collateral without thoroughly investigating the builder himself. The project was worthwhile. She had not considered that others might not have as altruistic goals as herself. She was forced to move from her home on F Street, where she had lived and worked for thirty-five years, into more modest quarters on Indiana Avenue.

Yet she was rich in more important matters. At this time in Belva's life she earned many honors. She received an honorary degree of Doctor of Laws from Syracuse University. In 1913 a group of Washington women commissioned a well-known artist of the day, Nellie Mathes Horne, to paint a life-size portrait of the country's first woman lawyer. Today it hangs in the National Museum of the nation's capital.

Three hundred prominent people gathered for the dedication dinner in the Willard Hotel. This was one of the few times Mrs. Lockwood was not asked to be the principal speaker for the occasion. Instead, she sat proudly beside her grandson, listening to others list her many accomplishments.

Still she was not through making public appearances. At the age of eighty-four she made her last trip to Europe as one of a group of eighteen American women asked by the State Department to present a peace message to the women of the world.

Nor did she forget her first crusade, women's rights. On May 9, 1914, she stood on the steps of the Capitol awaiting a parade of five hundred women demonstrators, members of the Congressional Union. When they had assembled, she joined the leaders of the organization to present a series of resolutions for voting reforms to Congress.

Her last political action was her campaign for the re-election of Woodrow Wilson as President of the United States. She hoped that Wilson could finally organize a world League of Nations that would prove her belief that arbitration could end wars. It was a blessing that she did not live to see the United States enter World War I.

In April of 1917 she became ill and was taken to George Washington Hospital. Three weeks later, on May 19, she died in her sleep.

The girl from Niagara County had accomplished much in her lifetime. She had never stopped fighting. She had taken upon herself the conscience of the world.

Bibliography

Baskin, Wade, and Runes, Richard N. *Dictionary of Black Culture.*
New York: Philosophical Library, 1973.

Brock, Peter. *Pacifism in the United States: From the Colonial Era to the
First World War.* Princeton, N.J.: Princeton University Press,
1965.

Dictionary of American Biography. "Lockwood, Belva Ann Bennett," by
Frances Fenton Park. 1933 ed., XI: 341.

Douglas, Emily Taft. *Remember the Ladies.* New York: G. P. Put-
nam's Sons, 1966.

Foundation of the Federal Bar Association with the cooperation of
the National Geographic Society of Washington, D.C. *Equal
Justice Under Law.* 1965 (distributed by Grosset & Dunlap).

Kerr, Laura. *The Girl Who Ran for President.* New York: Thomas Nel-
son, 1947.

Lockwood, Belva A. "The Growth of Peace Principles and Methods
of Propogating Them." Paper presented to the Triennial
Woman's Council at Washington, D.C., February 28, 1895.

Lockwood, Belva A. "The Right of Women to Vote Guaranteed by
the Constitution: Memorial with the Moral and Constitutional
Argument in Support of Same." Introduced into the Senate of
the United States, January 23, 1871. Washington, D.C.: Universal Franchise Association, 1971.

Lockwood, Belva A. "Women of the American Bar." *The Illustrated
American Monthly*, July 1891.

Logan, Mary Simmerson. *The Part Taken by Women in American History.* New York: Arno Press (reprint of 1912 publication).

Shaw, Ronald E. *Erie Water West: A History of the Erie Canal, 1792–1854.* Lexington, Ky.: University of Kentucky Press, 1966.

Sloan, Irving J. *Blacks in America, 1492–1970.* Dobbs Ferry, N.Y.: Oceana Publications, 1971.

Smith, Page. *Daughters of the Promised Land.* Boston: Little Brown, 1970.

Stern, Madeleine B. *We the Women.* New York: Schulte Publishing Company, 1963.

Tremain, Rose. *The Fight for Freedom for Women.* New York: Ballantine Books, 1973.

Van Every, Dale. *Disinherited: The Lost Birthright of the American Indian.* New York: William Morrow, 1967.

Winner, Julia Hull. *Belva A. Lockwood.* Number 19 of the Occasional Contributions of the Niagara County Historical Society. 1969.